Whistling in the Dark

AN ABC THEOLOGIZED

FICTION

A Long Day's Dying
The Seasons' Difference
The Return of Ansel Gibbs
The Final Beast
The Entrance to Porlock
Lion Country
Open Heart
Love Feast
Treasure Hunt
The Book of Bebb
Godric
Brendan

NONFICTION

The Magnificent Defeat
The Hungering Dark
The Alphabet of Grace
Wishful Thinking: A Theological ABC
The Faces of Jesus
Telling the Truth: The Gospel as Tragedy,
Comedy and Fairy Tale
Peculiar Treasures: A Biblical Who's Who
The Sacred Journey
Now and Then
A Room Called Remember

Whistling in the Dark

AN ABC THEOLOGIZED

Frederick Buechner

Illustrations by Katherine A. Buechner

1817

Harper & Row, Publishers, San Francisco

Cambridge, Hagerstown, New York, Philadelphia, Washington
London, Mexico City, São Paulo, Singapore, Sydney

WHISTLING IN THE DARK: *An ABC Theologized.* Copyright © 1988 by
Frederick Buechner. Illustrations copyright © 1988 by Katherine A. Buechner. All rights reserved. Printed in the United States of America. No part
of this book may be used or reproduced in any manner whatsoever without written permission except in the case of brief quotations embodied
in critical articles and reviews. For information address Harper & Row,
Publishers, Inc., 10 East 53rd Street, New York, NY 10022. Published
simultaneously in Canada by Fitzhenry & Whiteside Limited, Toronto.

FIRST EDITION

Library of Congress Cataloging-in-Publication Data

Buechner, Frederick,
  Whistling in the dark.

  1. Mediations. I. Title.
BV4832.2.B823   1988   200   87-45690
ISBN 0-061176-6

88 89 90 91 92 HC 10 9 8 7 6 5 4 3 2 1

To
The Dudley Knot

Contents

Introduction

A few years ago I wrote a book called *Wishful Thinking: A Theological ABC,* in which I took as many great religious words as happened to occur to me at the time and tried to say something I hoped would be entertaining and useful about what I believed they meant. Since then I have occasionally thought of other words I could have put in if I'd had my wits about me, and they are the ones that fill these pages. I used up almost all of the overtly theological ones the first time round, so most of these are just plain words which I've tried to say something more or less theological about. Faith is a kind of whistling in the dark, it seems to me, and these somewhat antic and most undefinitive definitions are in a way the same thing—an attempt to keep the spirits up while peering through the shadows for some glimmer of Meaning.

A word about the dedication is in order too. Dudley Knott was a friend of mine. Some friends are more or less replaceable with other friends, but he was not. He was an Englishman of great style, elegance, wit, and one of a kind. He could make you laugh till you cried. He had a tender heart. He walked with his shoulders back and his Greek fisherman's hat set square. He spent several days in Disneyland once trying to find out if it was possible to shoot Mickey Mouse from the tower of Cinderella's Castle. His favorite drink was half Dubonnet, half gin, no ice, and when his ashes were buried at sea in a box wrapped with the Union Jack, that was the libation that his friend Peter Black poured into the sea after them.

During the last winter of his life—he died on March 5, 1986—his eyesight got so bad that he could barely see to read so I started reading books to him. We did *The Man Who Was Thursday* and *The Aspern Papers*, among others. His wife Katty was usually there. So were his friends Edward Caulkins and Grenville Emmet. The winter following his death we started having the readings again, joined this time by his friend Douglas Auchincloss. For lack of anything more sensible we called ourselves The Dudley Knot, to whom, with Dudley himself of course, who was no mean whistler in the dark in his own right, these pages are dedicated. What he left us was not just our memories of him but our friendship, through him, with each other.

ABORTION

Speaking against abortion, someone has said, "No one should be denied access to the great feast of life," to which the rebuttal, obviously enough, is that life isn't much of a feast for the child born to people who don't want it or can't afford it or are one way or another incapable of taking care of it and will one way or another probably end up abusing or abandoning it.

And yet, and yet. Who knows what treasure life may hold for even such a child as that, or what a treasure even such a child as that may grow up to become? To bear a child even under the best of circumstances, or to abort a child even under the worst—the risks are hair-raising either way and the results incalculable.

How would Jesus himself decide, he who is hailed as Lord of Life and yet who says that it is not the ones who, like an abortionist, can kill the body we should fear but the ones who can kill body and soul together the way only the world into which it is born can kill the unloved, unwanted child (Matthew 10:28)?

There is perhaps no better illustration of the truth that in an imperfect world there are no perfect solutions. All we can do, as Luther said, is *sin bravely,* which is to say (a) know that neither to have the child nor not to have the child is without the possibility of tragic consequences for everybody yet (b) be brave in knowing also that not even that can put us beyond the forgiving love of God.

ADOLESCENCE

The ancient Druids are said to have taken a special interest in in-between things like mistletoe, which is neither quite a plant nor quite a tree, and mist, which is neither quite rain nor quite air, and

1

dreams which are neither quite waking nor quite sleep. They believed that in such things as those they were able to glimpse the
mystery of two worlds at once.

Adolescents can have the same glimpse by looking in the full-
length mirror on back of the bathroom door. The opaque glance
and the pimples. The fancy new nakedness they're all dressed up
in with no place to go. The eyes full of secrets they have a strong
hunch everybody is on to. The shadowed brow. Being not quite a
child and not quite a grown-up either is hard work, and they look
it. Living in two worlds at once is no picnic.

One of the worlds, of course, is innocence, self-forgetfulness,
openness, playing for fun. The other is experience, self-conscious-
ness, guardedness, playing for keeps. Some of us go on straddling
them both for years.

The rich young ruler of the Gospels comes to mind (Matthew
19:16–22). It is with all the recklessness of a child that he asks Jesus
what he must do to be perfect. And when Jesus tells him to give
everything to the poor, it is with all the prudence of a senior vice-
president of Morgan Guaranty that he walks sadly away.

We become fully and undividedly human, I suppose, when we
discover that the ultimate prudence is a kind of holy recklessness,
and our passion for having finds peace in our passion for giving,
and playing for keeps is itself the greatest fun. Once this has happened and our adolescence is behind us at last, the delight of the
child and the sagacity of the Supreme Court Justice are largely indistinguishable.

ADVENT

The house lights go off and the footlights come on. Even the
chattiest stop chattering as they wait in darkness for the curtain to
rise. In the orchestra pit, the violin bows are poised. The conductor
has raised his baton.

In the silence of a midwinter dusk there is far off in the deeps of it somewhere a sound so faint that for all you can tell it may be only the sound of the silence itself. You hold your breath to listen.

You walk up the steps to the front door. The empty windows at either side of it tell you nothing, or almost nothing. For a second you catch a whiff in the air of some fragrance that reminds you of a place you've never been and a time you have no words for. You are aware of the beating of your heart.

The extraordinary thing that is about to happen is matched only by the extraordinary moment just before it happens. Advent is the name of that moment.

The Salvation Army Santa Claus clangs his bell. The sidewalks are so crowded you can hardly move. Exhaust fumes are the chief fragrance in the air, and everybody is as bundled up against any sense of what all the fuss is really about as they are bundled up against the windchill factor.

But if you concentrate just for an instant, far off in the deeps of you somewhere you can feel the beating of your heart. For all its madness and lostness, not to mention your own, you can hear the world itself holding its breath.

AGING

When you hit sixty or so, you start having a new feeling about your own generation. Like you they can remember the Trilon and Perisphere, Lum and Abner, ancient Civil War veterans riding in open cars at the rear of Memorial Day parades, the Lindbergh kidnapping, cigarettes in flat fifties which nobody believed then could do any more to you than cut your wind. Like you they know about blackouts, Bond Rallies, A-stickers, Kilroy was Here. They remember where they were when the news came through that FDR was dead of a stroke in Warm Springs, and they could join you in singing "Bei Mir Bist Du Schön" and "The Last Time I Saw Paris." They wept at Spencer Tracy with his legs bitten off in *Captains Courageous*.

As time goes by, you start picking them out in crowds. There aren't as many of them around as there used to be. More likely than not, you don't say anything, and neither do they, but something seems to pass between you anyhow. They have come from the same beginning. They have seen the same sights along the way. They are bound for the same end and will get there about the same time you do. There are some who by the looks of them you wouldn't invite home for dinner on a bet, but they are your *compagnons de voyage* even so. You wish them well.

It is sad to think that it has taken you so many years to reach so obvious a conclusion.

ALCOHOLICS ANONYMOUS

Alcoholics Anonymous or A.A. is the name of a group of men and women who acknowledge that addiction to alcohol is ruining their lives. Their purpose in coming together is to give it up and help others do the same. They realize they can't pull this off by themselves. They believe they need each other, and they believe they need God. The ones who aren't so sure about God speak instead of their Higher Power.

When they first start talking at a meeting, they introduce themselves by saying, "I am John. I am an alcoholic," "I am Mary. I am an alcoholic," to which the rest of the group answers each time in unison, "Hi, John," "Hi, Mary." They are apt to end with the Lord's Prayer (q.v.) or the Serenity Prayer. Apart from that they have no ritual. They have no hierarchy. They have no dues or budget. They do not advertise or proselytize. Having no buildings of their own, they meet wherever they can.

Nobody lectures them, and they do not lecture each other. They simply tell their own stories with the candor that anonymity makes possible. They tell where they went wrong and how day by day they are trying to go right. They tell where they find the strength and understanding and hope to keep trying. Sometimes one of them will take special responsibility for another—to be available at any hour of day or night if the need arises. There's not much more to it than that, and it seems to be enough. Healing happens. Miracles are made.

You can't help thinking that something like this is what the Church is meant to be and maybe once was before it got to be Big Business. Sinners Anonymous. "I can will what is right but I cannot do it," is the way Saint Paul put it, speaking for all of us. "For I do not do the good I want, but the evil I do not want is what I do" (Romans 7:19).

"I am me. I am a sinner."

"Hi, you."

Hi, every Sadie and Sal. Hi, every Tom, Dick, and Harry. It is the forgiveness of sins, of course. It is what the Church is all about.

No matter what far place alcoholics end up in, either in this country or virtually anywhere else, they know that there will be an A.A. meeting nearby to go to and that at that meeting they will find strangers who are not strangers to help and to heal, to listen to the truth and to tell it. That is what the Body of Christ is all about.

Would it ever occur to Christians in a far place to turn to a Church nearby in hope of finding the same? Would they find it? If not, you wonder what is so Big about the Church's Business.

ALGEBRAIC PREACHING

$x + y = z$. If you know the value of one of the letters, you know something. If you know the value of two, you can probably figure out the whole thing. If you don't know the value of any, you don't know much.

Preachers tend to forget this. "Accept Jesus Christ as your personal Lord and Savior and be saved from your sins," or something like that, has meaning and power and relevance only if the congregation has some notion of what, humanly speaking, sin is, or being saved is, or who Jesus is, or what accepting him involves. If preachers make no attempt to flesh out these words in terms of everyday human experience (maybe even their own) but simply repeat with variations the same old formulas week after week, then the congregation might just as well spend Sunday morning at home with the funnies.

The blood atonement. The communion of saints. The Holy Ghost. If people's understanding of theological phrases goes little deeper than their dictionary or catechetical definitions, then to believe in them has just about as much effect on their lives as to believe that Columbus discovered America in 1492 or that E = mc².

Coming home from church one snowy day, Emerson wrote, "The snow was real but the preacher spectral." In other words nothing he heard from the pulpit suggested that the preacher was a human being more or less like everybody else with the same dark secrets and high hopes, the same doubts and passions, the same weaknesses and strengths. Undoubtedly he preached on matters like sin and salvation but without ever alluding to the wretched, lost moments or the glad, liberating moments of his own life or anybody else's.

There is perhaps no better proof for the existence of God than the way year after year he survives the way his professional friends promote him. If there are people who remain unconvinced, let them tune in their TVs to almost any of the big-time pulpit-pounders almost any Sunday morning of the year.

ANIMALS

"Out of the ground the Lord God formed every beast of the field and every bird of the air, and brought them to the man to see what he would call them; and whatever the man called every living creature, that was its name" (Genesis 2:19). Following Adam's lead we say *that* is the elephant and the albatross, *that* is the weasel and the goldfish. What or who they really are we do not know because they do not tell. They do not tell because they lack what is either the gift or the curse of speech depending on your point of view. Perhaps another reason they do not tell is that they do not know.

The marmalade cat dozing among the nasturtiums presumably doesn't think of herself as a marmalade cat or anything else for that matter. She simply is what she is and what she does. Whether she's mating under the moon or eviscerating a mouse or gazing into empty space, she seems to make herself up from moment to moment as she goes along.

Humans live largely inside their heads from which they tell the rest of their bodies what to do except for occasional passionate moments when the tables are turned. Animals, on the other hand, do not seem compartmentalized that way. Everything they are is in every move they make. When a dachshund takes a shine to you, it is not likely to be because he has thought it over ahead of time. Or in spite of certain reservations. Or in expectation of certain benefits. It seems to be just because it feels to him like a good idea at the time. Such as he is, he gives himself to you hook, line, and sinker, the bad breath no less than the frenzied tail and the front paws climbing the air. Needless to say the whole picture can change in a flash if you try to make off with his dinner, but for the moment his entire being is an act of love bordering on the beatific.

"Ask the animals, and they will teach you," Job says to his foul-weather friends. Innocence, as above, is one of their lessons, but the one Job has in mind is another, i.e., "that in [the Lord's] hand is the life of every creature and the breath of all mankind" (Job 12:7,10). When the ravens came and fed Elijah bread and meat by the brook Cherith (1 Kings 17:6), we're told they did it because the Lord commanded them to. However, I suspect that since, in spite of Poe, ravens are largely unverbal, the Lord caused the sight of the old man to be itself the command the way the smell of breakfast is a command to be hungry or the sound of your best friend on the stair a command to rejoice.

Elijah sat there all by himself—bald, on the run, in danger of starving to death. If the ravens could have talked, they would probably have tried to talk either the Lord or themselves out of doing anything about it. As it was, there was simply nothing for it but to bring him two squares a day till he moved on somewhere else.

The sleek, black birds and the bony, intractable prophet—since all life is one life, to save another is to save yourself, and with their wings, and beaks, and throbbing birds' hearts all working at once, the ravens set about doing it.

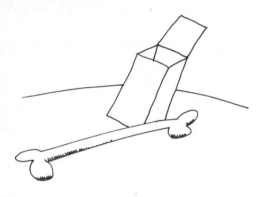

ANOREXIA

Nothing for breakfast. A diet soda for lunch. Maybe a little lettuce with low calorie dressing for supper or once in a while, when everybody has gone to bed, a binge on ice cream which you get rid of in the bathroom later. Relentless exercise. Obsession with food, cooking great quantities of it for everybody except yourself. In time you come to look like a victim of Dachau—the sunken eyes and hollow cheeks, the marionette arms and calfless legs. If you are a woman, you stop menstruating. If you are told your life itself is in jeopardy, it makes no difference because not even dying is as fearsome as getting fat, a view that the combined industries of fashion, dietetic food, and advertising all endorse. In every respect but this, you may be as sane as everybody else. In this, you are mad as a hatter.

Anorexia seems to be a modern disease, but old phrases like "pining away" and "wasting away" suggest it may have been around unnamed· for a long time. Nobody seems to know what it's all about though there are endless theories. Young anorexics want to strike free of parental control, they say, and where does it assume a more elemental form than in "Take a bite for Mummy, a bite for Daddy"? So that is where they draw the battle line. The more desperately they are urged to eat, the more desperately they resist. Their bodies are their last citadel, and they are prepared to defend them literally to the death. Yet on the other side of it, of course, they desperately need Mummy and Daddy and are scared stiff of the very independence they are fighting to achieve.

The craving to be free and independent. The craving to be taken care of and safe. The magic of the sickness is that it meets both these cravings at once. By not eating you take your stand against the world that is telling you what to do. By not eating you make your body so much smaller, lighter, weaker that in effect it becomes a child's body again, and the world flocks to your rescue. Is something like this at the heart of it?

Most anorexics are young women. Feeling that a male-dominated world has given them no models for what full womanhood means, do they believe that the golden key to that Wonderland garden is to make themselves as little as Alice had to in order to pass through the tiny curtained door? Who can say for sure?

But at least one thing is sure. By starving themselves, anorexics are speaking symbolically, and by trying above all else to make them start eating again, their families are in their own fashion speaking back the same way. Far beneath the issue of food there are, on both sides, unspoken issues of love, trust, fear, loss, separation. Father and mother, brother and sister, they are all of them afflicted together, acting out in pantomime a complex, subterranean drama whose nature they are at best only dimly aware of. And so, one way or another, are we all.

"Therefore, putting away falsehood, let every one speak the truth with his neighbor, for we are members one of another," says the author of Ephesians (4:25), and that is the heart of the matter.

I need you. I need to be myself. I am afraid. I am angry. I am in pain. Hear me. Help me. Let me try to help you. Let us love one another. If we would only speak the truth to one another—

parents and children, friends and enemies, husbands and wives, strangers and lovers—we would no longer have to act out our deepest feelings in symbols that none of us understand.

In our sickness, stubbornness, pride, we starve ourselves for what we hunger for above all else. "Speaking the truth in love" is another phrase from Ephesians (4:15). It is the only cure for the anorexia that afflicts us all.

ANXIETY

"Have no anxiety about anything," Paul writes to the Philippians. In one sense it is like telling a woman with a bad head cold not to sniffle and sneeze so much or a lame man to stop dragging his feet. Or maybe it is more like telling a wino to lay off the booze or a compulsive gambler to stay away from the track.

Is anxiety a disease or an addiction? Perhaps it is something of both. Partly, perhaps, because you can't help it, and partly because for some dark reason you choose not to help it, you torment yourself with detailed visions of the worst that can possibly happen. The nagging headache turns out to be a malignant brain tumor. When your teenage son fails to get off the plane you've gone to meet, you see his picture being tacked up in the post office among the missing and his disappearance never accounted for. As the latest mid-East crisis boils, you wait for the TV game show to be interrupted by a special bulletin to the effect that major cities all over the country are being evacuated in anticipation of nuclear attack. If Woody Allen were to play your part on the screen, you would roll in the aisles with the rest of them, but you're not so much as cracking a smile at the screen inside your own head.

Does the terrible fear of disaster conceal an even more terrible hankering for it? Do the accelerated pulse and the knot in the stomach mean that, beneath whatever their immediate cause, you are acting out some ancient and unresolved drama of childhood? Since the worst things that happen are apt to be the things you don't see coming, do you think there is a kind of magic whereby, if you only *can* see them coming, you will be able somehow to prevent them from happening? Who knows the answer? In addition to Novocain and indoor plumbing, one of the few advantages of living in the twentieth century is the existence of psychotherapists, and if you can locate a good one, maybe one day you will manage to dig up an answer that helps.

But answer or no answer, the worst things will happen at last even so. "All life is suffering" says the first and truest of the Buddha's Four Noble Truths, by which he means that sorrow, loss, death await us all and everybody we love. Yet "the Lord is at hand. Have no anxiety about anything," Paul writes, who was evidently in prison at the time and with good reason to be anxious about everything, "but in everything by prayer and supplication with thanksgiving let your requests be made known to God."

He does not deny that the worst things will happen finally to all of us, as indeed he must have had a strong suspicion they were soon to happen to him. He does not try to minimize them. He does not try to explain them away as God's will or God's judgment or God's method of testing our spiritual fiber. He simply tells the Philippians that in spite of them—even in the thick of them—they are to keep in constant touch with the One who unimaginably transcends the worst things as he also unimaginably transcends the best.

"In everything," Paul says, they are to keep on praying. Come Hell or high water, they are to keep on asking, keep on thanking, above all keep on making themselves known. He does not promise them that as a result they will be delivered from the worst things any more than Jesus himself was delivered from them. What he promises them instead is that "the peace of God, which passes all understanding, will keep your hearts and your minds in Christ Jesus."

The worst things will surely happen no matter what—that is to be understood—but beyond all our power to understand, he writes, we will have peace both in heart and in mind. We are as sure to be in trouble as the sparks fly upward, but we will also be "in Christ," as he puts it. Ultimately not even sorrow, loss, death can get at us there.

is the sense in which he dares say without risk of occa-
sioning ironic laughter, "Have no anxiety about anything." Or, as
he puts it a few lines earlier, "Rejoice in the Lord always. Again I
will say, Rejoice!" (Philippians 4:4–7).

APOLOGISTS

C. S. Lewis once said something to the effect that no Christian
doctrine ever looked so threadbare to him as when he had just
finished successfully defending it. The reason is not hard to find.

In order to defend the faith successfully—which is the business
of apologists—they need to reduce it to a defendable size. It is easier
to hold a fortress against the enemy than to hold a landscape. They
try to make each doctrine as it comes along sound as logical and
plausible as they can. The trouble, of course, is that by and large
logic and plausibility are not the heart of the matter, and therefore
apologists are apt to end up proclaiming a faith that may be quite
persuasive on paper but is difficult to imagine either them or anyone
else getting very excited about.

The other danger is that apologists put so much effort into what
they do that they may end up not so much defending the faith
because they believe it is true as believing the faith is true because
they have worked so hard and long to defend it.

ARMS RACE

Before Hiroshima you looked at the world and thought how sad
it would be when your last day finally came and you'd have to
leave it behind for good. There has been a new twist to the sadness
since. It is possible now that the world's last day may come before
ours does—only a little while before but long enough. Maybe we
will be the ones to be left behind.

"Lovely the woods, waters, meadows, combes, vales, / All the
air things wear that build this world," Gerard Manley Hopkins

wrote. Maybe it will be they, not we, who have to say goodbye—
the meadows sere and radioactive, the waters lifeless, the woods
without leaves or birds or squirrels to dither or kids to carve their
names into the bark of birches, and all the air things wear in August
as chill, grey, silent as a Vermont November.

The two great powers seem to operate under the assumption (a)
that the other one wants either to destroy it or to take it over and
(b) that in order to prevent such a thing from happening, there is
no price too high to pay. A six year old can see that the assumption
is of course insane. Maybe you can see it better at six than at sixty.
Even in the unlikely event that (a) is true, (b) is not. The one price
that is too high to pay for saving what you love is the destruction
of what you love.

Deep down, we all know that. Granted a preview of what things
would look like, including ourselves, after a thermonuclear ex-
change or two, it is hard to believe that anybody outside the mental
ward would claim it was worth it. Not even the President. Not
even the General Secretary. Not even the highest-flying hawk on
either side. Yet the race to the death goes on with a life all its own.
There are thoughtful and good people as well as fools and villains
who believe in it and fight for it while the rest of us crouch like
children behind the bannister waiting to hear what fateful decision
the grown-ups downstairs will make.

"God, lover of souls, swaying considerate scales, / Complete thy
creature dear O where it fails," Father Hopkins writes at the end
of the same sonnet. You don't have to be religious to say Amen
to that. Weighed in any kind of scales, our incompleteness is clearly
in danger of sinking us once and for all. Not just the economic,
political, social life of the nations is being crushed under the weight
of their failure to find ways of sharing the planet in peace but the
secret inner lives of all of us.

No one can look at the creature we are without seeing that it
fails. Something crucial is missing within us and among us all right,
and it may well prove the end of us. But there are times when you
can almost believe that maybe it is only *just* missing. As much as
anybody, it was the children who brought an end to the madness

of Vietnam with their long hair and flowers, their filthy jeans and dreadful music and unconquerable persistence. Maybe others like them will save the day for us again. If the world has never lacked for damned fools, it has never lacked for holy fools either.

The anti-war rallies, the nuclear plant sit-ins, the love-ins, the peace marches—it wouldn't be the first time that the weak proved stronger than the strong and the foolish wiser than the wise or that the world was saved by the last kind of person anybody on earth would ever have dreamed could save it.

ART

"An old silent pond. / Into the pond a frog jumps. / Splash! Silence again." It is perhaps the best known of all Japanese haiku. No subject could be more humdrum. No language could be more pedestrian. Basho, the poet, makes no comment on what he is describing. He implies no meaning, message, or metaphor. He simply invites our attention to no more and no less than just this: the old pond in its watery stillness, the kerplunk of the frog, the gradual return of the stillness.

In effect he is putting a frame around the moment, and what the frame does is enable us to see not just something about the moment but the moment itself in all its ineffable ordinariness and particularity. The chances are that if we had been passing by when the frog jumped, we wouldn't have noticed a thing or, noticing it, wouldn't have given it a second thought. But the frame sets it off from everything else that distracts us. It makes possible a second thought. That is the nature and purpose of frames. The frame does not change the moment, but it changes our way of perceiving the moment. It makes us NOTICE the moment, and that is what Basho wants above all else. It is what literature in general wants above all else too.

From the simplest lyric to the most complex novel and densest drama, literature is asking us to pay attention. Pay attention to the frog. Pay attention to the west wind. Pay attention to the boy on the raft, the lady in the tower, the old man on the train. In sum, pay attention to the world and all that dwells therein and thereby learn at last to pay attention to yourself and all that dwells therein.

The painter does the same thing, of course. Rembrandt puts a frame around an old woman's face. It is seamed with wrinkles. The upper lip is sunken in, the skin waxy and pale. It is not a remarkable face. You would not look twice at the old woman if you found her sitting across the aisle from you on a bus. But it is a face so remarkably *seen* that it forces you to see it remarkably just as Cézanne makes you see a bowl of apples or Andrew Wyeth a muslin curtain blowing in at an open window. It is a face unlike any other face in all the world. All the faces in the world are in this one old face.

Unlike painters, who work with space, musicians work with time, with note following note as second follows second. Listen! says Vivaldi, Brahms, Stravinsky. Listen to this time that I have framed between the first note and the last and to these sounds in time. Listen to the way the silence is broken into uneven lengths between the sounds and to the silences themselves. Listen to the scrape of bow against gut, the rap of stick against drumhead, the rush of breath through reed and wood. The sounds of the earth are like music, the old song goes, and the sounds of music are also like the sounds of the earth, which is of course where music comes from. Listen to the voices outside the window, the rumble of the furnace, the creak of your chair, the water running in the kitchen sink. Learn to listen to the music of your own lengths of time, your own silences.

Literature, painting, music—the most basic lesson that all art teaches us is to stop, look, and listen to life on this planet, including our own lives, as a vastly richer, deeper, more mysterious business than most of the time it ever occurs to us to suspect as we bumble along from day to day on automatic pilot. In a world that for the most part steers clear of the whole idea of holiness, art is one of the few places left where we can speak to each other of holy things.

Is it too much to say that Stop, Look, and Listen is also the most basic lesson that the Judeo-Christian tradition teaches us? Listen to history is the cry of the ancient prophets of Israel. Listen to social injustice, says Amos; to head-in-the-sand religiosity, says Jeremiah; to international treacheries and power-plays, says Isaiah; because it is precisely through them that God speaks his word of judgment and command.

And when Jesus comes along saying that the greatest command of all is to love God and to love our neighbor, he too is asking us to pay attention. If we are to love God, we must first stop, look, and listen for him in what is happening around us and inside us. If we are to love our neighbors, before doing anything else we must *see* our neighbors. With our imagination as well as our eyes, that is to say like artists, we must see not just their faces but the life behind and within their faces. Here it is love that is the frame we see them in.

In a letter to a friend Emily Dickinson wrote that "Consider the lilies of the field" was the only commandment she never broke. She could have done a lot worse. Consider the lilies. It is the *sine qua non* of art and religion both.

AWE

I remember seeing a forest of giant redwoods for the first time. There were some small children nearby, giggling and chattering and pushing each other around. Nobody had to tell them to quiet down as we entered. They quieted down all by themselves. Everybody did. You couldn't hear a sound of any kind. It was like coming into a vast, empty room.

Two or three hundred feet high the redwoods stood. You had to crane your neck back as far as it would go to see the leaves at the top. They made their own twilight out of the bright California day. There was a stillness and stateliness about them that seemed to become part of you as you stood there stunned by the sight of them. They had been growing in that place for going on two thousand years. With infinite care they were growing even now. You could feel them doing it. They made you realize that all your life you had been mistaken. Oaks and ashes, maples and chestnuts

and elms you had seen for as long as you could remember, but never until this moment had you so much as dreamed what a Tree really was.

"Behold the man," Pilate said when he led Jesus out where everybody could see him. He can't have been much to look at after what they'd done to him by then, but my guess is that, even so, there suddenly fell over that mob a silence as awed as ours in the forest when for the first time in their lives they found themselves looking at a Human Being.

BEATITUDES

If we didn't already know but were asked to guess the kind of people Jesus would pick out for special commendation, we might be tempted to guess one sort or another of spiritual hero—men and women of impeccable credentials morally, spiritually, humanly, and every which way. If so, we would be wrong. Maybe those aren't the ones he picked out because he felt they didn't need the shot in the arm his commendation would give them. Maybe they're not the ones he picked out because he didn't happen to know any. Be that as it may, it's worth noting the ones he did pick out.

Not the spiritual giants but "the poor in spirit" as he called them, the ones who spiritually speaking have absolutely nothing to give and absolutely everything to receive like the Prodigal telling his father "I am not worthy to be called thy son" only to discover for the first time all he had in having a father.

Not the champions of faith who can rejoice even in the midst of suffering but the ones who mourn over their own suffering because they know that for the most part they've brought it down on themselves, and over the suffering of others because that's just the way it makes them feel to be in the same room with them.

Not the strong ones but the meek ones in the sense of the gentle ones, i.e., the ones not like Caspar Milquetoast but like Charlie Chaplin, the little tramp who lets the world walk over him and yet, dapper and undaunted to the end, somehow makes the world more human in the process.

Not the ones who are righteous but the ones who hope they will be someday and in the meantime are well aware that the distance they still have to go is even greater than the distance they've already come.

Not the winners of great victories over Evil in the world but the ones who, seeing it also in themselves every time they comb their hair in front of the bathroom mirror, are merciful when they find it in others and maybe that way win the greater victory.

Not the totally pure but the "pure in heart," to use Jesus' phrase, the ones who may be as shop-worn and clay-footed as the next one but have somehow kept some inner freshness and innocence intact.

Not the ones who have necessarily found peace in its fullness but the ones who, just for that reason, try to bring it about wherever and however they can—peace with their neighbors and God, peace with themselves.

Jesus saved for last the ones who side with Heaven even when any fool can see it's the losing side and all you get for your pains is pain. Looking into the faces of his listeners, he speaks to them directly for the first time. "Blessed are you," he says.

You can see them looking back at him. They're not what you'd call a high-class crowd—peasants and fisherfolk for the most part, on the shabby side, not all that bright. It doesn't look as if there's a hero among them. They have their jaws set. Their brows are furrowed with concentration.

They are blessed when they are worked over and cursed out on his account he tells them. It is not his hard times to come but theirs he is concerned with, speaking out of his own meekness and mercy, the purity of his own heart.

(Matthew 5:1–12)

BEAUTY

Beauty is to the spirit what food is to the flesh. A glimpse of it in a young face, say, or an echo of it in a song fills an emptiness in you that nothing else under the sun can. Unlike food, however, it is something you never get your fill of. It leaves you always aching with longing not so much for more of the same as for whatever it is, deep within and far beyond both it and yourself, that makes it beautiful.

"The beauty of holiness" is how the Psalms name it (Psalm 29:2) and "As the hart panteth after the water brooks, so panteth my soul after thee" (Psalm 42:1) is the way they describe the ache and the longing.

BELIEVING

Prepositions can be very eloquent. A man is "in" architecture or a woman is "in" teaching, we say, meaning that is what they do weekdays and how they make enough money to enjoy themselves the rest of the time. But if we say they are "into" these things, that is another story. "Into" means something more like total immersion. They live and breathe what they do. They take it home with them nights. They can't get enough of it. To be "into" books means that just the sight of a signed first edition of *Alice in Wonderland* sets your heart pounding. To be "in" books means selling them at B. Dalton's.

Along similar lines, New Testament Greek speaks of believing "into" rather than believing "in." In English we can perhaps convey the distinction best by using either "in" or no preposition at all.

Believing in God is an intellectual position. It need have no more effect on your life than believing in Freud's method of interpreting dreams or the theory that Sir Francis Bacon wrote *Romeo and Juliet*.

Believing God is something else again. It is less a position than a journey, less a realization than a relationship. It doesn't leave you cold like believing the world is round. It stirs your blood like believing the world is a miracle. It affects who you are and what you do with your life like believing your house is on fire or somebody loves you.

We believe in God when for one reason or another we choose to do so. We believe God when somehow we run into God in a way that by and large leaves us no choice to do otherwise.

When Jesus says that whoever believes "into" him shall never die, he does not mean that to be willing to sign your name to the Nicene Creed guarantees eternal life. Eternal life is not the result of *believing in*. It is the experience of *believing*.

BOREDOM

As *acedia*, boredom is one of the Seven Deadly Sins. It deserves the honor.

You can be bored by virtually anything if you put your mind to it, or choose not to. You can yawn your way through *Don Giovanni* or a trip to the Grand Canyon or an afternoon with your dearest friend or a sunset. There are doubtless those who nodded off at the coronation of Napoleon or the trial of Joan of Arc or when Shakespeare appeared at the Globe in *Hamlet* or Lincoln delivered himself of a few remarks at Gettysburg. The odds are that the Sermon on the Mount had more than a few of the congregation twitchy and glassy-eyed.

To be bored is to turn down cold whatever life happens to be offering you at the moment. It is to cast a jaundiced eye at life in general including most of all your own life. You feel nothing is worth getting excited about because you are yourself not worth getting excited about.

To be bored is a way of making the least of things you often have a sneaking suspicion you need the most.

To be bored to death is a form of suicide.

BORN AGAIN

The phrase comes, of course, from a scene in John's Gospel where Jesus tells a Pharisee named Nicodemus that he will never see the Kingdom of God unless he is born again. Somewhat testily prodded by Nicodemus to make himself clearer, Jesus says, "That which is born of the flesh is flesh, and that which is born of the Spirit is spirit." In other words, spiritual rebirth by the power of the Holy Spirit is what Jesus is talking about.

He then goes one step further, playing on the word *pneuma,* which means both 'spirit' and 'wind' in Greek. "The wind blows where it will, and you hear the sound of it, but you do not know whence it comes or whither it goes; so it is with everyone who is born of the Spirit," he says (John 3:1–8). The implication seems to be that the kind of rebirth he has in mind is (a) elusive and mysterious and (b) entirely God's doing. There's no telling when it will happen or to whom.

Presumably those to whom it does happen feel themselves filled, as a sheer gift, with that love, joy, peace which Saint Paul singles out as the principal fruits of the experience. In some measure, however fleetingly, it is to be hoped that most Christians have had at least a taste of them.

Some of those who specifically refer to themselves as "Born Again Christians," however, seem to use the term in a different sense. You get the feeling that to them it means Super Christians. They are apt to have the relentless cheerfulness of car salesmen. They tend to be a little too friendly a little too soon and the women to wear more make-up than they need. You can't imagine any of them ever having had a bad moment or a lascivious thought or used a nasty word when they bumped their head getting out of the car. They speak a great deal about "the Lord" as if they have him in their hip pocket and seem to feel that it's no harder to figure out what he wants them to do in any given situation than to look up in Fanny Farmer how to make brownies. The whole shadow side of human existence—the suffering, the doubt, the frustration, the ambiguity—appears as absent from their view of things as litter from the streets of Disneyland. To hear them speak of God, he seems about as elusive and mysterious as a Billy Graham rally at Madison Square Garden, and on their lips the Born Again experience often sounds like something we can all make happen any time we want to, like fudge, if only we follow their recipe.

It is not for anybody to judge the authenticity of the Born Again's spiritual rebirth or anybody else's, but my guess is that by the style and substance of their witnessing to it, the souls they turn on to Christ are apt to be fewer in number than the ones they turn off.

BROTHERS

Cain murdered Abel. Jacob cheated Esau. Joseph's brothers sold him for twenty shekels and would probably have paid twice that to get him out of their hair. The Prodigal's elder brother couldn't stand being in the same room with him even with a fatted calf for inducement. As the Bible presents it, one of the closest of all relationships is also one of the saddest.

Envy and fear are apparently near to the heart of it—one brother is afraid the other is loved more, favored more, given and forgiven more, gets away with more—but that doesn't seem enough of an explanation somehow. You have a sense of signals crossed, of opportunities missed, of messages unheard or unheeded, in short of love gone wrong. You can't help thinking what friends they might have been if they hadn't been enemies. Cain giving Abel a hand with the spring lambing. Jacob letting Esau have his pottage just for the hell of it.

We all have the same dark secrets and the same bright hopes. We come from the same place and are headed in the same direction. Above everything else maybe, we all want to be known by each other and to know each other. The U.S.S.R. and the U.S.A., the Arabs and the Israelis, the terrorists and the terrorized—we are all of us brothers, all of us sisters.

Yet from the way we manage things most of the time, who in a million years would ever guess it? Who can remain unmoved by the thought of how the world might be if we only managed things right?

CHANTING

It is a form of high-church Popery that is supposed to set mainline Protestant teeth on edge. It shouldn't.

Words wear out after a while, especially religious words. We've said them so many times. We've listened to them so often. They are like voices we know so well we no longer hear them.

When a prayer or a psalm or a passage from the Gospels is chanted, we hear the words again. We hear them in a new way. We remember that they are not only meaning but music and mystery. The chanting italicizes them. The prose becomes poetry. The prosaic becomes powerful.

Of course chanting wears out after a while too.

CHARISMATIC

Most of the time when we say people are charismatic, we mean simply that they have presence. Bill Cosby, Charles Manson, the Princess of Wales, Dr. Ruth Westheimer all have it in varying degrees and forms. So did Benito Mussolini and Mae West. You don't have to be famous to have it either. You come across it in children and nobodies. Even if you don't see such people enter a room, you can feel them enter. They shimmer the air like a hot asphalt road. Without so much as raising a finger, they make you sit up and take notice.

On the other hand, if you took Mother Teresa, or Francis of Assisi, or Mahatma Gandhi, or the man who risked his neck smuggling Jews out of Nazi Germany, and dressed them up to look like everybody else, nobody would probably notice them any more than they would the woman who can make your day just by dropping by to borrow your steam iron, or the high school commencement speaker who without any eloquence or special intelligence can bring tears to your eyes, or the people who can quiet an hysterical child or stop somebody's cracking headache just by touching them with their hands. These are the true charismatics, from the Greek word *charis* meaning 'grace'. According to Saint Paul, out of sheer graciousness God gives certain men and women extraordinary gifts or *charismata* such as the ability to heal, to teach, to perform acts of mercy, to work miracles.

These people are not apt to have presence, and you don't feel any special vibrations when they enter a room. But they are all in their own ways miracle-workers, and even if you don't believe in the God who made them that way, you believe in them.

CHILDHOOD

Saint Paul wrote, "When I was a child, I spoke like a child, I thought like a child, I reasoned like a child; when I became a man, I gave up childish things" (1 Corinthians 13:11). Surely he was right to do so. Childish people are people who cling on to the worst of childhood, who tend to go on being spoiled, selfish, unreasonable, quarrelsome, egocentric, afraid of the dark, scattered, helpless, and so on long past the point when they should have pulled themselves together and wised up. As the saint suggests, you don't automatically grow out of those things the way you do diapers and acne. You have to make a conscious effort to put them behind you. Until you do, you're not really grown-up even though you're president of a college or eligible for medicare.

But it was Jesus himself who said, "Truly I say to you, unless you turn and become like children, you will never enter the kingdom of heaven." In other words, childish no, childlike yes. The question is childlike *how*?

Jesus himself gave the clue. According to Matthew, he called a child to him as he spoke and said, "Whoever humbles himself like this child, he is the greatest in the kingdom of heaven" (Matthew 18:1–4). It's worth looking at that small boy Jesus pulled out of the crowd, evidently at random.

Jesus puts him in front of him perhaps, his hands on his shoulders so he won't make a run for it. The child stands there wide-eyed, more than a little scared, much more than a little embarrassed, toeing the dust. If it weren't for the honor of the thing, as in Lincoln's joke, he'd as soon have been left unnoticed. He wishes he'd had time to get the hair out of his eyes and button up his shirt, at least to spit out his bubblegum. He dreads being asked some question that he can't answer or even one that he can. He hopes he won't be told to do something beyond him. He'd give a lot as he waits there to be as tall as his big brother or as smart as his Uncle Joe. He wishes he were anything worth being or knew anything worth knowing. All he knows for sure is that when the man called him, he had to go.

Presumably something like that is what Jesus meant by humble. Not Uriah Heep. Not self-deprecating and obsequious like a waiter angling for a tip. But above all else, maybe, clear-sighted. When the chips were down, the small boy saw himself for what he was. He didn't pretend to be anything he wasn't if only because he knew he probably wouldn't get away with it. As far as is recorded, he didn't even open his mouth. He knew who his elders and betters were. He was ready to take whatever they had to give and only hoped they wouldn't hold the bubblegum against him. If he had a large capacity for being scared and embarrassed, he also had a large capacity for being pleasantly surprised. In any case, he came when he was called.

If it's the Kingdom of Heaven we're interested in, Jesus says, we've got to be childlike like that. It's not so much a prerequisite or condition as it is simply a practical expedient. It's like saying if it's a pleasant surprise you're interested in, you've got to come as you are and hold out your hands.

CHRISTMAS

The lovely old carols played and replayed till their effect is like a dentist's drill or a jack hammer, the bathetic banalities of the pulpit and the chilling commercialism of almost everything else, people spending money they can't afford on presents you neither need nor want, "Rudolph the Red-Nosed Reindeer," the plastic tree, the cornball crèche, the Hallmark Virgin. Yet for all our efforts, we've never quite managed to ruin it. That in itself is part of the miracle, a part you can see. Most of the miracle you can't see, or don't.

The young clergyman and his wife do all the things you do on Christmas Eve. They string the lights and hang the ornaments. They supervise the hanging of the stockings. They tuck in the children. They lug the presents down out of hiding and pile them under the tree. Just as they're about to fall exhausted into bed, the husband remembers his neighbor's sheep. The man asked him to feed them for him while he was away, and in the press of other matters that night he forgot all about them. So down the hill he goes through knee-deep snow. He gets two bales of hay from the barn and carries them out to the shed. There's a forty-watt bulb hanging by its cord from the low roof, and he lights it. The sheep huddle in a corner watching as he snaps the baling twine, shakes the squares of hay apart and starts scattering it. Then they come bumbling and shoving to get at it with their foolish, mild faces, the puffs of their breath showing in the air. He is reaching to turn off the bulb and leave when suddenly he realizes where he is. The winter darkness. The glimmer of light. The smell of the hay and the sound of the animals eating. Where he is, of course, is the manger.

He only just saw it. He whose business it is above everything else to have an eye for such things is all but blind in that eye. He who on his best days believes that everything that is most precious anywhere comes from that manger might easily have gone home to bed never knowing that he had himself just been in the manger. The world is the manger. It is only by grace that he happens to see this other part of the miracle.

Christmas itself is by grace. It could never have survived our own blindness and depredations otherwise. It could never have *happened* otherwise. Perhaps it is the very wildness and strangeness of the grace that has led us to try to tame it. We have tried to make it habitable. We have roofed it in and furnished it. We have reduced it to an occasion we feel at home with, at best a touching and beautiful occasion, at worst a trite and cloying one. But if the Christmas event in itself is indeed—as a matter of cold, hard fact— all it's cracked up to be, then even at best our efforts are misleading.

The Word become flesh. Ultimate Mystery born with a skull you could crush one-handed. Incarnation. It is not tame. It is not touching. It is not beautiful. It is uninhabitable terror. It is unthinkable darkness riven with unbearable light. Agonized laboring led to it, vast upheavals of intergalactic space, time split apart, a wrenching and tearing of the very sinews of reality itself. You can only cover your eyes and shudder before it, before *this:* "God of God, Light of Light, very God of very God . . . who for us and for our salvation," as the Nicene Creed puts it, "came down from heaven."

Came down. Only then do we dare uncover our eyes and see what we can see. It is the Resurrection and the Life she holds in her arms. It is the bitterness of death he takes at her breast.

COMEDY

"Blessed are you that weep now, for you shall laugh," Jesus says. That means not just that you shall laugh when the time comes but that you can laugh a little even now in the midst of the weeping because you know that the time is coming. All appearances to the contrary notwithstanding, the ending will be a happy ending. That is what the laughter is about. It is the laughter of faith. It is the divine comedy.

In the meantime you weep because if you have a heart to see it with, the world you see is in a thousand ways heartbreaking. Only the heartless can look at it unmoved, and that is presumably why Jesus says, "Woe to you that laugh now, for you shall mourn and weep," meaning a different sort of laughter altogether—the laughter of callousness, mockery, indifference. You can laugh like that only if you turn your back on the suffering and need of the world, and perhaps for you the time for weeping comes when you see the suffering and need too late to do anything about them, like the specters of the dead that Jacob Marley shows old Scrooge as they reach out their spectral hands to try to help the starving woman and her child but are unable to do so now because they are only shadows.

The happiness of the happy ending—what makes the comedy so rich—is the suggestion that ultimately even the callous and indifferent will take part in it. The fact that Jesus says they too will weep and mourn before they're done seems to mean that they too will grow hearts at last, the hard way, and once that happens, the sky is the limit.

COMMUNION OF SAINTS

At the altar table, the overweight parson is doing something or other with the bread as his assistant stands by with the wine. In the pews, the congregation sits more or less patiently waiting to get into the act. The church is quiet. Outside, a bird starts singing. It's nothing special, only a handful of notes angling out in different directions. Then a pause. Then a trill or two. A chirp. It is just warming up for the business of the day, but it is enough.

The parson and his assistant and the usual scattering of senior citizens, parents, teenagers are not alone in whatever they think they're doing. Maybe that is what the bird is there to remind them. In its own slapdash way the bird has a part in it too. Not to mention "Angels and Archangels and all the company of heaven" if the prayer book is to be believed. Maybe we should believe it. Angels and Archangels. Cherubim and seraphim. They are all in the act together. It must look a little like the great *jeu de son et lumière* at Versailles when all the fountains are turned on at once and the night is ablaze with fireworks. It must sound a little like the last movement of Beethoven's *Choral Symphony* or the Atlantic in a gale.

And "all the company of heaven" means everybody we ever loved and lost, including the ones we didn't know we loved until we lost them or didn't love at all. It means people we never heard of. It means everybody who ever did—or at some unimaginable time in the future ever will—come together at something like this table in search of something like what is offered at it.

Whatever other reasons we have for coming to such a place, if we come also to give each other our love and to give God our love, then together with Gabriel and Michael, and the fat parson, and Sebastian pierced with arrows, and the old lady whose teeth don't fit, and Teresa in her ecstasy, we are the communion of saints.

CONVERSION

There are a number of conversions described in the New Testament. You think of Paul seeing the light on the road to Damascus, or the Ethiopian eunuch getting Philip to baptize him on the way from Jerusalem to Gaza. There is also the apostle Thomas saying, "My Lord and my God!" when he is finally convinced that Jesus is alive and whole again, not to mention the Roman centurion who witnessed the crucifixion saying, "Truly this man was the Son of God." All these scenes took place suddenly, dramatically, when they were least expected. They all involved pretty much of an about-face, which is what the word 'conversion' means. We can only imagine that they all were accompanied by a good deal of emotion.

But in this same general connection there are other scenes that we should also remember. There is the young man who, when Jesus told him he should give everything he had to the poor if he really wanted to be perfect as he said he did, walked sorrowfully away because he was a very rich young man. There is Nicodemus, who was sufficiently impressed with Jesus to go talk to him under cover of darkness and later to help prepare his body for burial, but who never seems to have actually joined forces with him. There is King Agrippa, who, after hearing Paul's impassioned defense of his faith, said, "Almost thou persuadest me to be a Christian." There is even Pontius Pilate, who asked, "What is truth?" under such circumstances as might lead you to suspect that just possibly, half without knowing it, he really hoped Jesus would be able to give him the answer, maybe even become for him the answer.

Like the conversions, there was a certain amount of drama about these other episodes too and perhaps even a certain amount of emotion though for the most part unexpressed. But of course in the case of none of them was there any about-face. Presumably all these people kept on facing more or less the same way they had been right along. King Agrippa, for instance, kept on being King Agrippa just as he always had. And yet you can't help wondering if somewhere inside himself, as somewhere also inside the rest of them, the "almost" continued to live on as at least a sidelong glance down a new road, the faintest itching of the feet for a new direction.

We don't know much about what happened to any of them after their brief appearance in the pages of Scripture, let alone what happened inside them. We can only pray for them, not to mention also for ourselves, that in the absence of a sudden shattering event, there was a slow underground process that got them to the same place in the end.

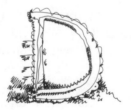

DARKNESS

The Old Testament begins with darkness, and the last of the Gospels ends with it.

"Darkness was upon the face of the deep," Genesis says. Darkness was where it all started. Before darkness, there had never been anything other than darkness, void and without form.

At the end of John, the disciples go out fishing on the Sea of Tiberias. It is night. They have no luck. Their nets are empty. Then they spot somebody standing on the beach. At first they don't see who it is in the darkness. It is Jesus.

The darkness of Genesis is broken by God in great majesty speaking the word of creation. "Let there be light!" That's all it took.

The darkness of John is broken by the flicker of a charcoal fire on the sand. Jesus has made it. He cooks some fish on it for his old friends' breakfast. On the horizon there are the first pale traces of the sun getting ready to rise.

All the genius and glory of God are somehow represented by these two scenes, not to mention what Saint Paul calls God's foolishness.

The original creation of light itself is almost too extraordinary to take in. The little cook-out on the beach is almost too ordinary to take seriously. Yet if Scripture is to be believed, enormous stakes were involved in them both and still are. Only a saint or a visionary can begin to understand God setting the very sun on fire in the heavens, and therefore God takes another tack. By sheltering a spark with a pair of cupped hands and blowing on it, the Light of the World gets enough of a fire going to make breakfast. It's not apt to be your interest in cosmology or even in theology that draws you to it so much as it's the empty feeling in your stomach. You don't have to understand anything very complicated. All you're asked is to take a step or two forward through the darkness and start digging in.

DENOMINATIONS

There are Baptists, Methodists, Episcopalians. There are Presbyterians, Lutherans, Congregationalists. There are Disciples of Christ. There are Seventh-day Adventists and Jehovah's Witnesses. There are Moravians. There are Quakers. And that's only for starters. New denominations spring up. Old denominations split up and form new branches. The question is not, Are you a Baptist? but, What kind of a Baptist? It is not, Are you a member of the Presbyterian church? but Which Presbyterian church? A town with a population of less than five hundred may have churches of three or four denominations and none of them more than a quarter full on a good Sunday.

There are some genuine differences between them, of course. The methods of church government differ. They tend to worship in different forms all the way from chanting (q.v.), incense, and saints' days to a service that is virtually indistinguishable from a New England town meeting with musical interludes. Some read the Bible more literally than others. If you examine the fine print, you may even come across some relatively minor theological differences among them, some stressing one aspect of the faith, some stressing others. But if you were to ask the average member of any congregation to explain those differences, you would be apt to be met with a long, unpregnant silence. By and large they all believe pretty much the same things and are confused about the same things and keep their fingers crossed during the same parts of the Nicene Creed.

However, it is not so much differences like these that keep the denominations apart as it is something more nearly approaching team spirit. Somebody from a long line of Congregationalists would no more consider crossing over to the Methodists than a Red Sox fan would consider rooting for the Mets. And even bricks and mortar have a lot to do with it. Your mother was married in this church building and so were you, and so was your oldest son. Your grandparents are buried in the cemetery just beyond the Sunday School wing. What on earth would ever persuade you to leave all that and join forces with the Lutherans in their building down the street? So what if neither of you can pay the minister more than a pittance and both of you have as hard a time getting more than thirty to fill the sanctuary built for two hundred as you do raising money to cover the annual heating bill.

All the duplication of effort and waste of human resources. All the confusion about what The Church is, both within the ranks and without. All the counterproductive competition. All the unnecessarily empty pews and unnecessary expense. Then add to that the picture the Roman Catholic Church, still more divided from the Protestant denominations than they are from each other, and by the time you're through, you don't know whether to burst into laughter or into tears.

When Jesus took the bread and said, "This is my body which is broken for you" (1 Corinthians 11:24), it's hard to believe that even in his wildest dreams he foresaw the tragic and ludicrous brokenness of the Church as his body. There's no reason why everyone should be Christian in the same way and every reason to leave room for differences, but if all the competing factions of Christendom were to give as much of themselves to the high calling and holy hope that unites them as they do now to the relative inconsequentialities that divide them, the Church would look more like the Kingdom of God for a change and less like an ungodly mess.

DEPRESSION

One of the most precious of the Psalms seems to be one of the least known as well as one of the shortest. It is the 131st. "O LORD, my heart is not lifted up," is the way it begins, "my eyes are not raised too high; / I do not occupy myself with things too great and too marvelous for me."

To be in a state of depression is like that. It is to be unable to occupy yourself with anything much except your state of depression. Even the most marvelous thing is like music to the deaf. Even the greatest thing is like a shower of stars to the blind. You do not raise either your heart or your eyes to the heights because to do so only reminds you that you are yourself in the depths. Even if, like the Psalmist, you are inclined to cry out "O LORD," it is a cry like Jonah's from the belly of a whale.

"But I have calmed and quieted my soul," he continues then, and you can't help thinking that although maybe that's better than nothing, it's not much better. Depression is itself a kind of calm as in becalmed and a kind of quiet as in a quiet despair.

Only then do you discover that he is speaking of something entirely different. He says it twice to make sure everybody understands. "Like a child quieted at its mother's breast," he says, and then again "like a child that is quieted is my soul." A kind of blessed languor that comes with being filled and somehow also fulfilled; the sense that no dark time that has ever been and no dark time that will ever be can touch this true and only time; *shalom*—something like that is the calm and quiet he has found. And the Lord in whom he has found it is the Lady Mother of us all. It is from her breast that he has drunk it to his soul's quieting.

Finally he tells us that hope is what his mouth is milky with, hope which is to the hopelessness of depression what love is to the lovesickness and lovelornness of fear. "O Israel, hope in the Lord," he says, "from this time forth and for evermore." Hope like Israel. Hope for deliverance the way Israel hoped and you are already half delivered. Hope beyond hope, and—like Israel in Egypt, in Babylon, in Dachau—you hope also beyond the bounds of your own captivity, which is what depression is.

Hope in the Father who is the Mother, the Lady who is the Lord. Do not raise your eyes too high but lower them to that holy place within you where you are fed and quieted, to that innermost manger where you are yourself the Child.

DESCENT INTO HELL

There is an obscure passage in the First Epistle of Peter where the old saint writes that after the crucifixion, Jesus went and preached to "the spirits in prison, who formerly did not obey," (1 Peter 3:19–20) and it's not altogether clear just what spirits he had in mind. Later on, however, he is not obscure at all. "The gospel was preached even to the dead," he says, "that though judged in the flesh like men, they might live in the spirit like God" (1 Peter 4:5–6).

"He descended into Hell," is the way the Apostles' Creed puts it, of course. It has an almost blasphemous thud to it, sandwiched there between the muffled drums of "was crucified, dead, and buried" and the trumpet blast of "the third day he rose again from the dead." Christ of all people, in Hell of all places! It strains the imagination to picture it, the Light of the World making his way through the terrible dark to save whatever ones he can. Yet in view of what he'd seen of the world during his last few days in the thick of it, maybe the transition wasn't as hard as you might think.

The fancifulness of the picture gives way to what seems, the more you turn it over in your mind, the inevitability of it. Of course that is where he would have gone. Of course that is what he would have done. Christ is always descending and redescending into Hell.

He is talking not just to other people when he says you must be prepared to forgive not seven times but seventy times seven, and "Come unto me, all ye that labor and are heavy laden" is spoken to *all,* whatever they've done or left undone, whichever side of the grave their Hell happens to be on.

DIVORCE (*See* LAW OF LOVE.)

DREAMS

No matter how prosaic, practical, and ploddingly unimaginative we may be, we have dreams like everybody else. All of us do. In them even the most down-to-earth and pedestrian of us leave earth behind and go flying, not walking, through the air like pelicans. Even the most respectable go strolling along crowded pavements naked as truth. Even the confirmed disbelievers in an afterlife hold converse with the dead just as the most dyed-in-the-wool debunkers of the supernatural have adventures to make Madame Blavatsky's hair stand on end.

The tears of dreams can be real enough to wet the pillow and the passions of them fierce enough to make the flesh burn. There are times we dream our way to a truth or an insight so overwhelming that it startles us awake and haunts us for years to come. As easily as from room to room, we move from things that happened so long ago we had forgotten them to things lying ahead that may be waiting to happen or trying to happen still. On our way we are as likely to meet old friends as perfect strangers. Sometimes, inexplicably, we meet casual acquaintances who for decades haven't so much as once crossed our minds.

Freudians and Jungians, prophets and poets, philosophers, fortunetellers, and phonies all have their own claims about what dreams mean. Others claim they don't mean a thing. But there are at least two things they mean that seem incontrovertible.

One of them is that we are in constant touch with a world that is as real to us while we are in it, and has as much to do with who we are, and whose ultimate origin and destiny are as unknown and fascinating, as the world of waking reality. The other one is that our lives are a great deal richer, deeper, more intricately interrelated, more mysterious, and less limited by time and space than we commonly suppose.

People who tend to write off the validity of the religious experience in general and the experience of God in particular on the grounds that in the Real World they can find no evidence for such things should take note. Maybe the Real World is not the only reality, and even if it should turn out to be, maybe they are not really looking at it realistically.

DYING

The airport is crowded, noisy, frenetic. There are yowling babies, people being paged, the usual ruckus. Outside, a mixture of snow and sleet is coming down. The runways show signs of icing. Flight delays and cancellations are called out over the PA system together with the repeated warning that in view of recent events any luggage left unattended will be immediately impounded. There are more people than usual smoking at the various gates. The air is blue with it. Once aboard you peer through the windows for traces of ice on the wings and search the pancaked faces of the stewardesses for anything like the knot of anxiety you feel in your own stomach as they run through the customary emergency procedures. The great craft lumbers its way to the take-off position, the jets shrill. Picking up speed, you count the seconds till you feel lift-off. More than so many, you've heard, means trouble. Once airborne, you can hardly see the wings at all through the grey turbulence scudding by. The steep climb is rough as a Ford pick-up. Gradually it starts to even out. The clouds thin a little. Here and there you see tatters of clear air among them. The pilot levels off slightly. Nobody is talking. The calm and quiet of it are almost palpable. Suddenly, in a rush of light, you break out of the weather. Beneath you the clouds are a furrowed pasture. Above, no sky in creation was ever bluer.

Possibly the last take-off of all is something like that. When the time finally comes, you're scared stiff to be sure, but maybe by then you're just as glad to leave the whole show behind and get going. In a matter of moments, everything that seemed to matter stops mattering. The slow climb is all there is. The stillness. The clouds. Then the miracle of flight as from fathom upon fathom down you surface suddenly into open sky. The dazzling sun.

EARTH

For thousands upon thousands of years people couldn't see it whole—only as much of it at a time as there was between wherever they happened to be and the horizon. For most of them, the question of flatness or roundness must have seemed altogether irrelevant. Either way it was plainly enormous. Beyond the fields and the mountains there was the sea, and beyond the sea more fields, more mountains. Whatever wild ideas they had about how it came into being or who made it, they knew it had been around more or less forever. Just by looking at it you could tell that—the ancient rocks, the vast deserts. Nothing less than God himself could ever bring it to an end, and he didn't seem to be in any special hurry about it. In the meanwhile, though time and change eventually carried off everybody and everything else, it was as clear as anything was clear that at least the place they were carried off from was for keeps. Spring would follow winter like the ebb and flow of the tides. Life in one odd shape or another would keep going on and on, the old ones dying and the new ones being born.

Then suddenly pictures were taken from miles away, and we saw it at last for what it truly is. It is about the size of a dime. It is blue with swirls of silver. It shines. The blackness it floats in is so immense it seems almost miraculously not to have swallowed it up long since.

Seeing it like that for the first time, you think of Jesus seeing Jerusalem for the last time. The ass he's riding comes clipclopping around a bend in the road, and without warning there it is. His eyes fill with tears, as Luke describes it. "Would that even today you knew the things that make for peace," he says. "For the days shall come . . . " (Luke 19:41, 43). The holy city.

The holy earth. We must take such care of it. It must take such care of us. This side of Paradise, we are each of us so nearly all the other has. There is darkness beyond the dreams of avarice all around us. Among us there is just about enough light to get by.

EASTER

Christmas has a large and colorful cast of characters including not only the three principals themselves but the Angel Gabriel, the

Innkeeper, the Shepherds, the Heavenly Host, the Three Wise Men, Herod, the Star of Bethlehem, and even the animals kneeling in the straw. In one form or another we have seen them represented so often that we would recognize them anywhere. We know about the birth in all its detail as well as we know about the births of ourselves or our children, maybe moreso. The manger is as familiar as home. We have made a major production of it, and as minor attractions we have added the carols, the tree, the presents, the cards, Santa Claus, Ebeneezer Scrooge, and so on. With Easter it is entirely different.

The Gospels are far from clear as to just what happened. It began in the dark. The stone had been rolled aside. Matthew alone speaks of an earthquake. In the tomb there were two white-clad figures or possibly just one. Mary Magdalen seems to have gotten there before anybody else. There was a man she thought at first was the gardener. Perhaps Mary the mother of James was with her and another woman named Joanna. One account says Peter came too with one of the other disciples. Elsewhere the suggestion is that there were only the women and that the disciples, who were somewhere else, didn't believe the women's story when they heard it. There was the sound of people running, of voices. Matthew speaks of "fear and great joy." Confusion was everywhere. There is no agreement even as to the role of Jesus himself. Did he appear at the tomb or only later? Where? To whom did he appear? What did he say? What did he do?

It is not a major production at all, and the minor attractions we have created around it—the bunnies and baskets and bonnets, the dyed eggs—have so little to do with what it's all about that they neither add much nor subtract much. It's not really even much of a story when you come right down to it, and that is of course the power of it. It doesn't have the ring of great drama. It has the ring of truth. If the Gospel writers had wanted to tell it in a way to convince the world that Jesus indeed rose from the dead, they would presumably have done it with all the skill and fanfare they could muster. Here there is no skill, no fanfare. They seem to be telling it simply the way it was. The narrative is as fragmented, shadowy, incomplete as life itself. When it comes to just what happened, there can be no certainty. That something unimaginable happened, there can be no doubt.

The symbol of Easter is the empty tomb. You can't depict or domesticate emptiness. You can't make it into pageants and string it with lights. It doesn't move people to give presents to each other or sing old songs. It ebbs and flows all around us, the Eastertide. Even the great choruses of Handel's *Messiah* sound a little like a handful of crickets chirping under the moon.

He rose. A few saw him briefly and talked to him. If it is true, there is nothing left to say. If it is not true, there is nothing left to say. For believers and unbelievers both, life has never been the same again. For some, neither has death. What is left now is the emptiness. There are those who, like Magdalen, will never stop searching it till they find his face.

ENEMY

Cain hated Abel for standing higher in God's esteem than he felt he himself did so he killed him. King Saul hated David for stealing the hearts of the people with his winning ways and tried to kill him every chance he got. Saul of Tarsus hated the followers of Jesus because he thought they were blasphemers and heretics and made a career of rounding them up so they could be stoned to death like Stephen. By and large most of us don't have enemies like that anymore, and in a way it's a pity.

It would be pleasant to think it's because we're more civilized nowadays, but maybe it's only because we're less honest, open, brave. We tend to avoid fiery outbursts for fear of what they may touch off both in ourselves and the ones we burst out at. We smolder instead. If people hurt us or cheat us or stand for things we abominate, we're less apt to bear arms against them than to bear grudges. We stay out of their way. When we declare war, it is mostly submarine warfare, and since our attacks are beneath the surface, it may be years before we know fully the damage we have either given or sustained.

Jesus says we are to love our enemies and pray for them, meaning love not in an emotional sense but in the sense of willing their good, which is the sense in which we love ourselves. It is a tall order even so. The South African black love the lords of apartheid? The longtime employee who is laid off just before he qualifies for retirement with a pension love the people who call him in to break the news? The mother of the molested child love the molester? But when you see as clearly as that who your enemies are, at least you see your enemies clearly too.

You see the lines in their faces and the way they walk when they're tired. You see who their husbands and wives are maybe. You see where they're vulnerable. You see where they're scared. Seeing what is hateful about them, you may catch a glimpse also of where the hatefulness comes from. Seeing the hurt they cause you, you may see also the hurt they cause themselves. You're still light years away from loving them, to be sure, but at least you see how they are human even as you are human, and that is at least a step in the right direction. It's possible that you may even get to where you can pray for them a little, if only that God forgive them because you yourself can't, but any prayer for them at all is a major breakthrough.

In the long run, it may be easier to love the ones we look in the eye and hate, the enemies, than the ones whom—because we're as afraid of ourselves as we are of them—we choose not to look at at all.

FACES

Faces, like everything else, can be looked at and not seen. Walking down a sidewalk at rush hour or attending the World Series, you're surrounded by thousands of them, but they might as well be balloons at a political rally for all you notice them individually. Here and there one of them may catch your eye for a moment, but in another moment you've forgotten it. They are without personalities, without histories. There is nothing to remember them by. They are anonymous strangers. As far as you are concerned, they simply don't matter. They are too much to take in.

But the odds are that for at least one other person somewhere in the world each of them—even the unlikeliest—matters enormously, or mattered enormously once, or someday, with any luck, will come to matter. The pimply boy with the beginnings of a moustache, the fat girl eating popcorn, the old black in the baseball cap, the woman with no upper teeth, the suntanned blonde with the disagreeable mouth—if you set your mind to it, there's hardly a one of them you can't imagine somebody *loving* even, conceivably even yourself. If the fat girl were your kid sister, for instance. Or the old black your son. Or the pimply boy to grow up to be your father. Or the toothless woman to have been your first great

love. Each face you see has, or used to have, or may have yet, the power—out of all the other faces in creation—to make at least some one other person's heart skip a beat just by turning up in an old photograph album, maybe, or appearing unexpectedly at the front door.

Needless to say, it's easier to imagine it with some than with others. For all her good looks it's harder with the suntanned blonde than with the sweaty truck driver shooting a squirt of cut plug, but even with her you can probably manage it in the end. There's hardly a face coming at you down the supermarket aisle or up the subway escalator that you can't manage it with given the right set of circumstances, the right pair of eyes. You can see even the bitter faces in terms of what probably made them that way. You can see even the hostile, ugly faces in terms of what they must have been once before the world got to them, what they might have become if they'd gotten the breaks.

Every now and again, however, you come across faces that are too much for you. There are people it's impossible to imagine loving if only because they look so much as though they wouldn't let you even if you could. If there are faces of the blessed to be seen in this world, there are also faces of the damned. Maybe you can love them for precisely that reason then. Maybe you're the one who has to love them because nobody else ever has.

In any case, the next time you find yourself in a crowd with nothing better to do, it's a game worth playing.

FAMILY

The Human Family. It's a good phrase, reminding us not only that we come from the same beginning and are headed toward the same conclusion but that in the meantime our lives are elaborately and inescapably linked. A famine in one part of the world affects people in all parts of the world. An assassination in Dallas or Sarajevo affects everybody. No man is an island. It is well worth remembering.

But families have a way of being islands notwithstanding—the Flanagans as distinct from the Schwartzes and the Schwartzes never to be confused with the Cherbonneaus or the Riondas. You think of a row of houses on a street. The same drama is going on in all of them—the Human Drama—but in each of them a unique drama is also going on. Though the wood walls are so thin you can hear a baby's cry through them, they are solid enough to keep out the world. If in the Schwartzes' house the baby dies—or grows up and gets married by the rambler roses in the backyard—all the other families on the street rally round and do what they can. But it is in the Schwartzes' house alone that what happens happens fully. With the best will in the world, nobody on the outside can know the richness and mystery of it, the foreshadowings of it deep in the past, the reverberations of it far in the future. With the best will in the world, nobody on the inside can make it known.

It is not so much that things happen in a family as it is that the family is the things that happen in it. The family is continually becoming what becomes of it. It is every christening and every commencement, every falling in love, every fight, every departure and return. It is the moment at breakfast when for no apparent reason somebody gets up and leaves the table. It is the sound of the phone ringing in the middle of the night or the lying awake hours waiting for it to ring. It is the waves pounding the boardwalk to pieces and the undercurrents so deep beneath the surface that you're hardly aware of them.

A family is a web so delicately woven that it takes almost nothing to set the whole thing shuddering or even to tear it to pieces. Yet the thread it's woven of is as strong as anything on earth. Sixty years after his father's death, the old man can't bring himself to remember it, or to stop remembering. Even when the twenty-year-old daughter runs out and never comes back, she can hear the raised voices from downstairs as she's going to sleep a thousand miles away, and every year when the old birthdays or deathdays come by, she marks each of them as surely as she marks that the sun has gone under a cloud or the moon risen.

It is within the fragile yet formidable walls of your own family that you learn, or do not learn, what the phrase Human Family means.

FATHER

When a child is born, a father is born. A mother is born too, of course, but at least for her it's a gradual process. Body and soul, she has nine months to get used to what's happening. She becomes what's happening. But for even the best-prepared father, it happens all at once. On the other side of the plate-glass window, a nurse is holding up something roughly the size of a loaf of bread for him to see for the first time. Even if he should decide to abandon it forever ten minutes later, the memory will nag him to the grave. He has seen the creation of the world. It has his mark upon it. He has its mark upon him. Both marks are, for better or worse, indelible.

All sons, like all daughters, are prodigals if they're smart. Assuming the Old Man doesn't run out on them first, they will run out on him if they are to survive, and if he's smart he won't put up too much of a fuss. A wise father sees all this coming, and maybe that's why he keeps his distance from the start. He must survive too. Whether they ever find their way home again, none can say for sure, but it's the risk he must take if they're ever to find their way at all. In the meantime, the world tends to have a soft spot in its heart for lost children. Lost fathers have to fend for themselves.

Even as the father lays down the law, he knows that someday his children will break it as they need to break it if ever they're to find something better than law to replace it. Until and unless that happens, there's no telling the scrapes they will get into trying to lose him and find themselves. Terrible blunders will be made— disappointments and failures, hurts and losses of every kind. And they'll keep making them even after they've found themselves too, of course, because growing up is a process that goes on and on. And every hard knock they ever get knocks the father even harder still if that's possible, and if and when they finally come through more or less in one piece at the end, there's maybe no rejoicing greater than his in all creation.

It has become so commonplace to speak of God as "our Father" that we forget what an extraordinary metaphor it once was.

FEMALE

"So God created man in his own image, in the image of God he created him; male and female he created them" (Genesis 1:27). In other words the female as much as the male is a reflection of the Creator. They are created at the same time, and they are created equals. God blesses them and charges them together and gives the female, along with the male, dominion over the earth. In the next chapter, however, a different story is told. There God creates Adam first and only afterwards, realizing that "it is not good that the man should be alone," decides to make a helper for him, fashioning Eve out of one of Adam's ribs and calling her "Woman, because she was taken out of Man" (Genesis 2:18–22).

These two conflicting views of the female's role in the order of things scarcely need to be spelled out further, nor is it necessary to point out that generally speaking it is the second of them that has prevailed down through the centuries.

Little by little women have turned things pretty much around. They vote. They get elected heads of state. They excel in arts and professions that were once for men only. Some of the stuffiest mens' clubs accept them and virtually all of the most venerable mens' colleges. They are increasingly successful in getting equal pay for equal jobs. Major denominations ordain them. It has been a long, slow exodus, but finally it seems to be paying off.

Feminism can become another form of sexism. Knee-jerk feminists can match their macho counterparts in pig-headedness, aggressiveness, humorlessness, bigotry. Their shrill voices can make the head ache. When they refuse to read *King Lear* because it's full of sexist language and bar males from their lectures and demonstrations because they're males, their efforts are apt to be more counterproductive than otherwise. But no matter.

Prophets have always been strident and a little crazy. They've needed to be. The prophet Deborah wouldn't have beaten the tar out of the Canaanites by issuing directives from her living room any more than Moses would have gotten his people out of Egypt by writing letters to the *New York Times*.

FRIENDS

Friends are people you make part of your life just because you feel like it. There are lots of other ways people get to be part of each other's lives like being related to each other, living near each other, sharing some special passion with each other like P. G. Wodehouse or jogging or lepidopterology, and so on, but though all or any of those may be involved in a friendship, they are secondary to it.

Basically your friends are not your friends for any particular reason. They are your friends for no particular reason. The job you

do, the family you have, the way you vote, the major achievements
and blunders of your life, your religious convictions or lack of
them, are all somehow set off to one side when the two of you
get together. If you are old friends, you know all those things about
each other and a lot more besides, but they are beside the point.
Even if you talk about them, they are beside the point. Stripped,
humanly speaking, to the bare essentials, you are yourselves the
point. The usual distinctions of older-younger, richer-poorer,
smarter-dumber, male-female even, cease to matter. You meet with
a clean slate every time, and you meet on equal terms. Anything
may come of it or nothing may. That doesn't matter either. Only
the meeting matters.

"The Lord used to speak to Moses face to face, as a man speaks
to his friend," the Book of Exodus says (Exodus 33:11), and in the
Book of Isaiah it is God himself who says the same thing of Abraham. "Abraham, my friend," he calls him (Isaiah 41:8). It is a staggering thought.

The love of God. The mercy of God. The judgment of God.
You take the shoes off your feet and stand as you would before a
mountain or at the edge of the sea. But the *friendship* of God?

It is not something God does. It is something Abraham and God,
or Moses and God, do together. Not even God can be a friend all
by himself apparently. You see Abraham, say, not standing at all
but sitting down, loosening his prayer shawl, trimming the end off
his cigar. He is not being Creature for the moment, and God is
not being Creator. There is no agenda. They are simply being together, the two of them, and being themselves.

Is it a privilege only for patriarchs? Not as far as Jesus is concerned at least. "You are my friends," he says, "if you do what I
command you." The command, of course, is "to love one another,"
as he puts it. To be his friends, that is to say, we have to be each
other's friends, conceivably even lay down our lives for each other.
You never know (John 15:12–15). It is a high price to pay, and
Jesus does not pretend otherwise, but the implication is that it's
worth every cent.

FUNERAL

In Aramaic *talitha cumi* means "little girl, get up." It's the language Jesus and his friends probably used when they spoke to each other, so these may well be his actual words, among the very few that have come down to us verbatim. He spoke them at a child's funeral, the twelve-year-old daughter of a man named Jairus (Mark 5:35–43).

The occasion took place at the man's house. There was plenty of the kind of sorrow you expect when anybody that young dies. And that's one of the great uses of funerals surely, to be cited when people protest that they're barbaric holdovers from the past, that you should celebrate the life rather than mourn the death, and so on. Celebrate the life by all means but face up to the death of that life. Weep all the tears you have in you to weep because whatever may happen next, if anything does, this has happened. Something precious and irreplaceable has come to an end and something in you has come to an end with it. Funerals put a period after the sentence's last word. They close a door. They let you get on with your life.

The child was dead, but Jesus, when he got there, said she was only asleep. He said the same thing when his friend Lazarus died. Death is not any more permanent than sleep is permanent is what he meant apparently. That isn't to say he took death lightly. When he heard about Lazarus, he wept, and it's hard to imagine him doing any differently here. But if death is the closing of one door, he seems to say, it is the opening of another one. *Talitha cumi.* He took the little girl's hand, and he told her to get up, and she did. The mother and father were there, Mark says. The neighbors, the friends. It is a scene to conjure with.

Old woman, get up. Young man. The one you don't know how you'll ever manage to live without. The one you don't know how you ever managed to live with. Little girl. "Get up," he says.

The other use of funerals is to remind us of those two words. When the last hymn has been sung, the benediction given, and the immediate family escorted out a side door, they may be the best we have to make it possible to *get up* ourselves.

GAME

Games are supposed to build character. The Battle of Waterloo was won on the playing fields of Eton and all that. Healthy competition is supposed to be good for you.

Is competition ever healthy—the desire to do better, be better, look better than somebody else? Do you write better poetry or play better tennis or do better in business or stand in higher esteem generally, even in self-esteem, if your chief motivation is to be head of the pack? Even if you win the rat race, as somebody has said, are you any less a rat?

Who wants to win if somebody else has to lose? Who dares to lose if it's crucial to win?

"Ah, but it's not winning that counts. It's how you play the game," they say. Maybe neither of them counts. Maybe it's not competition but cooperation and comradeship that build the only character worth building. If it's by playing games together that we learn to win battles, maybe it's by playing, say, music together that we learn to avoid them.

There are moments when Saint Paul sounds like a competitor with a vengeance, but there are happily other moments as well. "Let us run with perseverance the race that is set before us," he says (Hebrews 12:1), where the object is not to get there first but just to get there. And "Fight the good fight," he says (1 Timothy 6:12), where it's not the fight to overcome the best of the competition that he's talking about but the fight to overcome the worst in ourselves.

GENTLEMAN/GENTLEWOMAN

By one definition they are people who have gone to the schools and colleges everybody's heard of, don't talk with their mouths full, avoid using *like* as a conjunction, don't make scenes in public, and so on. They are apt to turn up in such places as country clubs, the society pages, and restaurants in which proper dress is required. They may commit murder from time to time, but they rarely end up in the electric chair. If a child of yours marries one of them, you figure he or she has done all right. If they're usually no better than other people, they are usually no worse either. Or if they are, it at least doesn't show so much.

But there are gentlewomen and gentlemen in another sense who may be none of the above. They may speak atrocious English and get their clothes at rummage sales. They may leave their spoons in their coffee cups and douse their french fries with ketchup. There are some of them who, if they turned up at a country club, would be directed to the service entrance. Some are educated, and some barely made it through grade school. Some are captains of industry, and some pump gas for a living. But whatever the differences between them, the common denominator is even more striking.

"Gentle" is the key word, of course. Their table manners may be appalling, but their courtesy is instinctive. They let you take the seat by the window or have first go at the morning paper not because it's in Emily Post but because it's in their nature. They seem to be born knowing when to come around and when to stay away. If you have them over for supper, they know when it's time to go home. Their wit may be sharp, but it never cuts. Even in private they don't make scenes if they can possibly help it.

They have their hang-ups and abysses and blind spots like everybody else, but when Jesus said, "Blessed are the meek," if it wasn't exactly them he was talking about, the chances are it was people very much like them. (*See also* BEATITUDES.)

GHOST

What keeps ghosts going seems to be usually some ancient tragedy they can't cut loose from or some dramatic event they are perpetually reenacting or some unfinished business they never seem able to resolve. They are so shadowy that it's hard to believe they exist. Some of the more spectacular hauntings—cups and saucers flying through the air, midnight wailings, a haggard face at the window—suggest they may have grave doubts on the subject themselves. It seems to be that if they can only make somebody's hair stand on end, possibly their own even, it helps convince them they aren't just figments of their own imagination. They prefer deserted places because they feel deserted. They disappear at cockcrow because the idea of seeing themselves, or being seen, for what they truly are scares the daylights out of them.

If you want to see one, take a look in the mirror someday when you yourself are feeling particularly haggard and shadowy.

GOODBYE

A woman with a scarf over her head hoists her six year old up onto the first step of the school bus. "Goodbye," she says.

A father on the phone with his freshman son has just finished bawling him out for his poor grades. There is mostly silence at the other end of the line. "Well, goodbye," the father says.

When the girl at the airport hears the announcement that her plane is starting to board, she turns to the boy who is seeing her off. "I guess this is goodbye," she says.

The noise of the traffic almost drowns out the sound of the word, but the shape of it lingers on the old man's lips. He tries to look vigorous and resourceful as he holds out his hand to the other old man. "Goodbye." This time they say it so nearly in unison that it makes them both smile.

It was a long while ago that the words *God be with you* disappeared into the word *goodbye,* but every now and again some trace of them still glimmers through.

GOVERNMENT

It seems safe to say that if you were to take a confidential poll of the private citizens of the nations of the world, all but a handful of firebrands and crazies would come out in favor of peace at pretty much any price. On both sides of the Iron Curtain, in Islam as well as in Christendom and the Third World, they have their conflicting political systems, ideologies, and holy causes to be sure, but by and large they give the strong impression of asking little more than a chance to raise their children as best they can, keep the wolf from the door, have some fun when they're through working at the end of the day, find some sort of security against old age, and all such as that.

Their leaders, on the other hand, are continually delivering ultimatums to each other, plotting to confound each other any way they can manage it, spying on each other, vilifying each other, impugning each other's motives, spending billions on weapons to destroy each other, and all such as that.

If at this most basic level, governments don't reflect the dreams of the people they govern or serve their wills, you wonder what on earth governments are. Reading the papers, you get the sense of them as small, irascible groups within each capital—far more of them men than women—who behave in ways that under normal circumstances would land them in the slammer in no time flat. They seem to have a life and purpose of their own quite apart from the lives and purposes of anybody else. They are perpetually locked in desperate struggles with each other that have little if anything to do with the general human struggle to live and let live with as little fuss as possible. It's we ourselves who have given them the power to pull the whole world down on all our heads, and yet we seem virtually powerless to stop them.

We need governments to collect taxes, keep the roads in repair, maintain order in the streets and justice in the courts, etc., but we certainly don't need this. They don't pay us, we pay them, yet they're the ones who call the shots while the rest of us stand by with our knees knocking. Gulliver in all his travels never came across anything to equal it.

HATE

Hate is as all-absorbing as love, as irrational, and in its own way as satisfying. As lovers thrive on the presence of the beloved, haters revel in encounters with the one they hate. They confirm him in all their darkest suspicions. They add fuel to all his most burning animosities. The anticipation of them makes the hating heart pound. The memory of them can be as sweet as young love.

The major difference between hating and loving is perhaps that whereas to love somebody is to be fulfilled and enriched by the experience, to hate somebody is to be diminished and drained by it. Lovers, by losing themselves in their loving, find themselves, become themselves. Haters simply lose themselves. Theirs is the ultimately *consuming* passion.

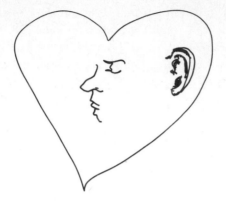

HEARING

If I can't see you for some reason but can only hear you, you don't exist for me in space, which is where seeing happens, but in time, which is where hearing happens. Your words follow one after the other the way tock follows tick. When I have only the sound of you to go by, I don't experience you as an object the way I would if you stood before me—something that I can walk around, inspect from all angles, more or less define. I experience you more the way I experience the beating of my own heart or the flow of my own thoughts. A deaf man coming upon me listening to you would think that nothing of importance was going on. But something of extraordinary importance is going on. I am taking you more fully into myself than I can any other way. Hearing you speak brings me by the most direct of all routes something of the innermost secret of who you are.

It is no surprise that the Bible uses hearing, not seeing, as the predominant image for the way human beings know God. They can't walk around him and take him in like a cathedral or an artichoke. They can only listen to time for the sound of him—to the good times and bad times of their own lives for the words which out of his innermost secrets he is addressing to, of all people, them.

HEAVEN

"And I saw the holy city, new Jerusalem, coming down out of heaven from God, prepared as a bride adorned for her husband; and I heard a great voice from the throne saying . . . 'Behold, I make all things new' " (Revelation 21:2–5).

Everything is gone that ever made Jerusalem, like all cities, torn apart, dangerous, heartbreaking, seamy. You walk the streets in peace now. Small children play unattended in the parks. No stranger goes by whom you can't imagine a fast friend. The city has become what those who loved it always dreamed and what in their dreams she always was. The *new* Jerusalem. That seems to be the secret of Heaven. The new Chicago, Leningrad, Hiroshima, Beirut. The new bus driver, hot-dog man, seamstress, hairdresser. The new you, me, everybody.

It was always buried there like treasure in all of us—the best we had it in us to become—and there were times you could almost see it. Even the least likely face, asleep, bore traces of it. Even the bombed-out city after nightfall with the public squares in a shambles and moonlight glazing the broken pavement. To speak of heavenly music or a heavenly day isn't always to gush but sometimes to catch a glimpse of something. "Death shall be no more, neither shall there be mourning nor crying nor pain any more," the Book of Revelation says. You can catch a glimpse of that too in almost anybody's eyes if you choose the right moment to look, even in animals' eyes.

If the new is to be born, though, the old has to die. It is the law of the place. For the best to happen, the worst must stop happening—the worst we are, the worst we do. But maybe it isn't as difficult as it sounds. It was a hardened criminal within minutes of death, after all, who said only, "Jesus, remember me," and that turned out to be enough. "This day you will be with me in Paradise" was the answer he just managed to hear.

HELP

As they're used psychologically, words like *repression, denial, sublimation, defense,* all refer to one form or another of the way human beings erect walls to hide behind both from each other and from themselves. You repress the memory that is too painful to deal with, say. You deny your weight problem. You sublimate some of your sexual energy by channeling it into other forms of activity more socially acceptable. You conceal your sense of inadequacy behind a defensive bravado. And so on and so forth. The inner state you end up with is a castle-like affair of keep, inner wall, outer wall, moat, which you erect originally to be a fortress to keep the enemy out but which turns into a prison where you become the jailer and thus your own enemy. It is a wretched and lonely place. You can't be what you want to be there or do what you want to do. People can't see through all that masonry to who you truly are, and half the time you're not sure you can see who you truly are yourself, you've been walled up so long.

Fortunately there are two words that offer a way out, and they're simply these: Help me. It's not always easy to say them—you have your pride after all, and you're not sure there's anybody you trust enough to say them to—but they're always worth saying. To another human being—a friend, a stranger? To God? Maybe it comes to the same thing.

Help me. They open a door through the walls, that's all. At least hope is possible again. At least you're no longer alone.

HOLOCAUST

It is impossible to think about it. It is impossible not to think about it. Nothing in history equals the horror of it. There is no way to imagine it. There is no way to speak of it without diminishing it. Thousands upon thousands of them were taken away in Nazi Germany during the Second World War. They were gassed. Their corpses were burned. Many were old men. Many were small children. Many were women. They were charged with nothing except being Jews. In the end there were apparently something like six million of them who died, six thousand thousands.

Anyone who claims to believe in an all-powerful, all-loving God without taking into account this devastating evidence either that God is indifferent or powerless, or that there is no God at all, is playing games.

Anyone who claims to believe in the inevitable perfectibility of the human race without taking this into account is either a fool or a lunatic.

That many of the people who took part in the killings were professing Christians, not to mention many more who knew about the killings but did nothing to interfere, is a scandal which the Church of Christ perhaps does not deserve to survive.

For people who don't believe in God, suffering can be understood simply as part of the way the world works. The Holocaust is no more than an extreme example of the barbarities that human beings have been perpetrating on each other since the start. For people who do believe in God, it must remain always a dark and awful mystery.

If Love itself is really at the heart of all, how can such things happen? What do such things mean? The Old Testament speaks of the elusive figure of the Suffering Servant who though "despised and rejected of men" and brutally misused has nonetheless willingly "borne our griefs and carried our sorrows" and thereby won an extraordinary victory in which we all somehow share (Isaiah 52:13–53:12). The New Testament speaks of the Cross, part of whose meaning is that even out of the worst the world can do, God is still able to bring about the best.

But all such explanations sound pale and inadequate before the gas chambers of Buchenwald and Ravensbrück, the ovens of Treblinka.

HOMOSEXUAL

One of the many ways that we are attracted to each other is sexually. We want to touch and be touched. We want to give and receive pleasure with our bodies. We want to know each other in our full nakedness, which is to say in our full humanness, and in the moment of passion to become one with each other. Whether it is our own gender or the other that we are chiefly attracted to seems a secondary matter. There is a female element in every male just as there is a male element in every female, and most people if they're honest will acknowledge having been at one time or another attracted to both.

To say that morally, spiritually, humanly, homosexuality is always bad seems as absurd as to say that in the same terms heterosexuality is always good, or the other way round. It is not the object of our sexuality that determines its value but the inner nature of our sexuality. If (a) it is as raw as the coupling of animals, at its worst it demeans us and at its best still leaves our deepest hunger for each other unsatisfied. If (b) it involves some measure of kindness, understanding, affection as well as desire, it can become an expression of human love in its fullness and can thus help to complete us as humans. Whatever our sexual preference happens to be, both of these possibilities are always there. It's not whom you go to bed with or what you do when you get there that matters so much. It's what besides sex you are asking to receive, and what besides sex you are offering to give.

Here and there the Bible condemns homosexuality in the sense of (a) just as under the headings of adultery and fornication it also condemns heterosexuality in the sense of (a). On the subject of homosexuality in the sense of (b), it is as silent as it is on the subject of sexuality generally in the sense of (b). The great commandment is that we are to love one another—responsibly, faithfully, joyfully—and presumably the biblical view is implied in that.

Beyond that, "Love is strong as death," sings Solomon in his song. "Many waters cannot quench love, neither can floods drown it" (Song of Solomon 8:6–7). Whoever you are and whomever you desire, the passion of those lines is something you are quick to recognize.

IMAGINATION

Even a thousand miles inland you can smell the sea and hear the mewing of gulls if you give thought to it. You can see in your mind's eye the living faces of people long dead or hear in the mind's ear the United States Marine Band playing "The Stars and Stripes Forever." If you work at it, you can smell the smell of autumn leaves burning or taste a chocolate malted. You don't have to be asleep to dream dreams either. There are those who can come up with dramas laid twenty thousand leagues under the sea or take a

little girl through a looking glass. Imagining is perh
humans get to creating something out of nothing tl
said to. It is a power that to one degree or another
or can develop, like whistling. Like muscles, it can b
through practice and exercise. Keep at it until you ca
your grandfather's voice, for instance, or feel the r
when you open the four hundred and fifty degree o

If imagination plays a major role in the creation
plays a major one also in the appreciation of it. It
read imaginatively as well as to write imaginatively
know what's really going on. A good novelist helps
stimulating our imaginations—sensory detail is espe
this regard such as the way characters look and dre
and smells of the places they live and so on—but th
do our part. It is especially important to do it in rea
Be the man who trips over a suitcase of hundred dol
in the field he's plowing if you want to know what
of Heaven is all about (Matthew 13:44). Listen to
"Come unto me, all ye that labor and are heavy la
give you rest" (Matthew 11:28) until you can *hear* hi
to know what faith is all about.

If you want to know what loving your neighbor
look at them with more than just your eyes. The ba
down for the night on the hot air grating. The two
ing like birds in the sandbox. The bride as she walks
on her father's arm. The old man staring into space
home TV room. Try to know them for who they a
skins. Hear not just the words they speak but the v
not speak. Feel what it's like to be who they are—
bird because for the moment you are a bird, trying
as you move slowly into the future with all eyes up

When Jesus said, "All ye that labor and are heavy
seeing the rich as well as the poor, the lucky as well a
the idle as well as the industrious. He was seeing th
wedding day. He was seeing the old man in front

was seeing all of us. The highest work of the imagination is to have eyes like that.

INNOCENCE

"Be wise as serpents and innocent as doves," Jesus told the disciples when he sent them off to spread the good news (Matthew 10:16). In other words, you can be both. Innocence doesn't mean being Little Red Ridinghood. You can know which side is up. You can have been around. Certainly the disciples had—fishermen, husbands and fathers, a tax collector—and Jesus thought them capable of being innocent even so. But they were to be sharp-eyed, not wide-eyed. He was sending them out "as sheep in the midst of wolves," he said, and they would need their wits about them. They were to be smart sheep.

Innocent people may be up to their necks in muck with the rest of us, but the mark of their innocence is that it never seems to stick to them. Things may be rotten all around them, but they preserve a curious freshness. Even when, like the disciple Peter, they are guilty of tragic flaws and failures, you feel that some inner purity remains untouched. Everybody knew, for instance, that the woman who washed Jesus' feet in Simon the Pharisee's house was no better than she ought to be, but as she dried them with her hair and kissed them, apart from Simon there was no one there, least of all Jesus, who would have dreamed of holding it against her (Luke 7:36–49).

JOBS

Jobs are what people do for a living, many of them for eight hours a day, five days a week, minus vacations, for most of their lives. It is tragic to think how few of them have their hearts in it. They work mainly for the purpose of making money enough to enjoy their moments of not working.

If not working is the chief pleasure they have, you wonder if they wouldn't do better just to devote themselves to that from the start. They would probably end up in bread-lines or begging, but even so the chances are they would be happier than pulling down a good salary as an insurance agent or a dental technician or a cab driver and hating every minute of it.

"What does man gain by all the toil at which he toils under the sun?" asks the Preacher (Ecclesiastes 1:3). If he's in it only for the money, the money is all he gains, and when he finally retires, he may well ask himself if it was worth giving most of his life for. If he's doing it for its own sake—if he enjoys doing it and the world needs it done—it may very possibly help to gain him his own soul.

JOGGING

It is supposed to be good for the heart, the lungs, the muscles, and physical well-being generally. It is also said to produce a kind of euphoria known as joggers' high.

The look of anguish and despair that contorts the faces of most of the people you see huffing and puffing away at it by the side of the road, however, is striking. If you didn't know directly from them that they are having the time of their lives, the chances are you wouldn't be likely to guess it.

JOKE

A good joke is one that catches you by surprise, God's for instance. Who would have guessed that Israel of all nations would be the one God picked or Sarah would have Isaac at the age of ninety or the Messiah would turn up in a manger? Who could possibly see the duck-billed platypus coming or Saint Simeon Stylites or the character currently occupying the pulpit at First Presbyterian? The laugh in each case results from astonished delight at the sheer unexpectedness of the thing.

Satan's jokes, on the other hand, you can usually spot a mile off. As soon as the serpent came slithering up to Adam and Eve, almost anybody could tell that the laugh was going to be on them. That a person as blameless, upright, and well-heeled as Job was bound to have the rug pulled out from under him before he was through. That Faust being Faust was sure to be conned out of his soul. And so on.

In the last analysis, the only one who gets much of a kick out of Satan's jokes is Satan himself. With God's, however, even the most hardened cynics and bitterest pessimists have a hard time repressing an occasional smile, and when he really gets going, he has pretty much the whole creation rolling in the aisles.

JUSTICE

If you break a good law, justice must be invoked not only for goodness' sake but for the good of your own soul. Justice may consist of paying a price for what you've done or simply of the painful knowledge that you deserve to pay a price, which is payment enough. Without one form of justice or the other, the result is ultimately disorder and grief for you and everybody. Thus justice is itself not unmerciful.

Justice also does not preclude mercy. It makes mercy possible. Justice is the pitch of the roof and the structure of the walls. Mercy is the patter of rain on the roof and the life sheltered by the walls. Justice is the grammar of things. Mercy is the poetry of things.

The Cross says something like the same thing on a scale so cosmic and full of mystery that it is hard to grasp. As it represents what one way or another human beings are always doing to each other, the death of that innocent man convicts us as a race and we deserve the grim world that over the centuries we have made for ourselves. As it represents what one way or another we are always doing not so much to God above us somewhere as to God within us and among us everywhere, we deserve the very godlessness we have brought down on our own heads. That is the justice of things.

But the Cross also represents the fact that goodness is present even in grimness and God even in godlessness. That is why it has become the symbol not of our darkest hopelessness but of our brightest hope. That is the mercy of things. Granted who we are, perhaps we could have seen it no other way.

KING

You think of the newly anointed King David conquering unconquerable Jerusalem and crowning his triumph by bringing into it the ark of God as all the people made merry with lyres, harps, tambourines, castanets, and cymbals. You think of the Pope himself proclaiming Charlemagne Emperor and *augustus* on Christmas Day and all Rome going mad with enthusiasm. You think of Shakespeare's Henry the Fifth comforting his troops on the eve of Agincourt and of the *grands levers* of Louis the Fourteenth which rivaled in splendor the rising of the sun. Muffled drums and vast crowds of mourners followed the deaths of kings, and the peal of bells and dancing in the streets their births. The person of the king was so sacred that affronts upon him were punished with the most horrible of torments, and his touch had the power to heal.

Passionate loyalty, adoration, terror, awe—no words are perhaps too strong to describe the feelings evoked in his subjects by the mere sight of him, and it's no wonder. He held the power of life and death over them. Their destiny was in his keeping. He defended the kingdom against all enemies both from within and from without. He *was* the kingdom. If he rejoiced, it rejoiced with him. If he was angry, the earth trembled and the crops might fail.

"Who is this King of glory? The LORD of hosts, he is the King of glory!" proclaims the Psalmist (24:10). This rich metaphor is used again and again in Scripture. Yahweh alone was King over Israel, the prophets thundered: to be feared, to be loved, above all else to be obeyed. When the people decided they wanted a king of flesh and blood like all the other nations, Samuel warned them that the consequences would be tragic (1 Samuel 8:4–18), and history proved him correct in every particular. In the long run Israel as king and kingdom vanished from history altogether.

When Jesus entered Jerusalem for the last time, it was as King and Son of David that his followers hailed him. If it was a king like David the conquering hero that they were looking for, they were of course bitterly disappointed. What they got was a king like David the father, who, when he heard of his treacherous son's death, went up to his chamber and wept. "Would I had died instead of thee, O Absalom, my son, my son!" he cried out. They were the most kingly words he ever uttered and an uncanny foreshadowing of events some thousand years off.

KNOWLEDGE

Knowing something or somebody isn't the same as knowing *about* them. More than just information is involved. The knower doesn't simply add to his mental store and go his way otherwise unchanged. To know is to participate in, to become imbued with, for better or worse to be affected by. When you really *know* a person or a language or a job, the knowledge becomes part of who you are. It gets into the bloodstream. That is presumably why the Tree of the Knowledge of Good and Evil was the one tree Adam and Eve were warned to steer clear of.

When in their innocence they knew only Good, they could be only good. As soon as they knew Evil too, a whole new glittering vista opened up before them. Next to obedience appeared the possibility of disobedience, next to faithfulness faithlessness, next to love lust, next to kindness, cruelty, and so on. Even when they chose the good way, their knowledge of the evil way remained as a conscious and by no means unattractive alternative, preventing them except on the rarest occasions from being good wholeheartedly. And when they chose the evil way, their knowledge of good tended to turn even the sweetness of forbidden fruit to ashes in their mouths. Thus they became the hapless hybrids their descendants have been ever since. It was the curse God had tried to spare them. The serpent did his work well.

According to Thomas Aquinas, God can know Evil by pure intelligence without becoming tainted by it the way a doctor can know the nature of disease without becoming diseased. Humans, on the other hand, not being pure intelligences but creatures of flesh and blood inhabiting a world of space and time, can know only through the likes of experience, experiment, will, imagination, and once they start knowing Evil that way, the fat is in the fire.

Once you know Evil, is there any way to get rid of it? The Cross of Christ suggests a solution. By a creative act, God transformed the torturing to death of an innocent person into a source of new life for innumerable people. With help from God and from each other, maybe we can work something like the same white magic on the evil within ourselves. For instance, if we're not ready yet to change passionate hate for somebody into passionate love, we can start by wishing people well whom we don't much like, and it's hard to do that for long without developing a kind of grudging affection for them along the way. It's not much, but it's at least a start.

LAW OF LOVE

Jesus said that the one supreme law is that we are to love God with all our hearts, minds, souls, and our neighbors as ourselves. "On these two commandments depend all the law and the prophets" is the way he put it (Matthew 22:40), meaning that all lesser laws are to be judged on the basis of that supreme one. In any given situation, the lesser law is to be obeyed if it is consistent with the Law of Love and superseded if it isn't.

The law against working on the sabbath is an example found in the Gospels. If it is a question of whether or not you should perform the work of healing people on the sabbath, Jesus' answer is clear. Of *course* you should heal them is his answer. Obviously healing rather than preserving your own personal piety is what the Law of Love would have you do. Therefore you put the lesser law aside.

The Mosaic law against murder is an example of precisely the opposite kind. In this case, far from setting the lesser law aside, you radicalize it. That is to say if we are above all else to love our neighbors, it is not enough simply not to kill them. We must also not lose our tempers at them, insult them, and call them fools, Jesus says (Matthew 5:21–22).

A legalistic religion like the Pharisees' is in some ways very appealing. All you have to do in any kind of ethical dilemma is look it up in the book and act accordingly. Jesus, on the other hand, says all you have to do is love God and your neighbors. That may seem more appealing still until, in dilemma after dilemma, you try to figure out just how to go about doing it.

The difficulty is increased when you realize that by loving God and your neighbors, Jesus doesn't mean loving as primarily a feeling. Instead he seems to mean that whether or not any feeling is involved, loving God means honoring and obeying and staying in constant touch with God, and loving your neighbors means acting in their best interests no matter what, even if personally you can't stand them.

Nothing illustrates the difficulty of all this better than the situation of a man and woman who for one reason or another decide to get divorced but take their faith seriously enough to want to do what's right. Jesus himself comes out strongly against it. "What God has joined together, let not man put asunder" is the way he puts it (Mark 10:9). In one place he is quoted as acknowledging that unchastity on the woman's part may be considered justifiable grounds, but he is clearly not happy about it (Matthew 5:31–32,

Mark 10:2–9). In other words, insofar as Jesus lays down the law on the subject, divorce is out.

But presumably his laws are to be judged by the same standards as the next person's.

Who knows what has gone amiss in the marriage? Who knows which partner, if either, is more at fault? Who knows what the long-term results either of splitting up or of staying together will be? If there are children, who can say which will be better for them, those small neighbors we are commanded to love along with the rest of them? Will it be living on with married parents whose constant battling, say, can do terrible things to a child? Or will it be going off with one divorced parent or the other and falling victim thereby to all the feelings of rejection, guilt, loss which can do equally terrible things to a child if not moreso?

What would the Law of Love have you do in a situation so complex, precarious, fateful? How can you best serve, in love, the best interests of the husband or wife you are miserable with, your children, yourself, God? There is no book to look up the answer in. There is only your own heart and whatever by God's grace it has picked up in the way of insight, honesty, courage, humility, and, maybe above everything else, compassion.

LENT

In many cultures there is an ancient custom of giving a tenth of each year's income to some holy use. For Christians, to observe the forty days of Lent is to do the same thing with roughly a tenth of each year's days. After being baptized by John in the river Jordan, Jesus went off alone into the wilderness where he spent forty days asking himself the question what it meant to be Jesus. During Lent, Christians are supposed to ask one way or another what it means to be themselves.

If you had to bet everything you have on whether there is a God or whether there isn't, which side would get your money and why?

When you look at your face in the mirror, what do you see in it that you most like and what do you see in it that you most deplore?

If you had only one last message to leave to the handful of people who are most important to you, what would it be in twenty-five words or less?

Of all the things you have done in your life, which is the one you would most like to undo? Which is the one that makes you happiest to remember?

Is there any person in the world, or any cause, that, if circumstances called for it, you would be willing to die for?

If this were the last day of your life, what would you do with it?

To hear yourself try to answer questions like these is to begin to hear something not only of who you are but of both what you are becoming and what you are failing to become. It can be a pretty depressing business all in all, but if sackcloth and ashes are at the start of it, something like Easter may be at the end.

LONELINESS

That you can be lonely in a crowd, maybe especially there, is readily observable. You can also be lonely with your oldest friends, or your family, even with the person you love most in the world. To be lonely is to be aware of an emptiness which it takes more than people to fill. It is to sense that something is missing which you cannot name.

"By the waters of Babylon, there we sat down and wept, when we remembered Zion," sings the Psalmist (137:1). Maybe in the end it is Zion that we're lonely for, the place we know best by longing for it, where at last we become who we are, where finally we find home.

LORD'S PRAYER

In the Episcopal order of worship, the priest sometimes introduces the Lord's Prayer with the words, "Now, as our Savior Christ hath taught us, we are bold to say . . ." The word *bold* is worth thinking about. We do well not to pray the prayer lightly. It takes guts to pray it at all. We can pray it in the unthinking and perfunctory way we usually do only by disregarding what we are saying.

"Thy will be done" is what we are saying. That is the climax of the first half of the prayer. We are asking God to be God. We are asking God to do not what we want but what God wants. We are asking God to make manifest the holiness that is now mostly hidden, to set free in all its terrible splendor the devastating power that is now mostly under restraint. "Thy kingdom come . . . on earth" is what we are saying. And if that were suddenly to happen, what then? What would stand and what would fall? Who would be welcomed in and who would be thrown the Hell out? Which if any of our most precious visions of what God is and of what human beings are would prove to be more or less on the mark and which would turn out to be phony as three-dollar bills? Boldness indeed. To speak those words is to invite the tiger out of the cage, to unleash a power that makes atomic power look like a warm breeze.

You need to be bold in another way to speak the second half. Give us. Forgive us. Don't test us. Deliver us. If it takes guts to face the omnipotence that is God's, it takes perhaps no less to face the impotence that is ours. We can do nothing without God. We can have nothing without God. Without God we are nothing.

It is only the words "Our Father" that make the prayer bearable. If God is indeed something like a father, then as something like children maybe we can risk approaching him anyway.

MALE

Males are strong, daring, aggressive. Females are gentle, prudent, sensitive. That's the way it was always supposed to be. If a particnular male didn't fit the picture by nature, he generally tended to let on that he did. He wasn't free to be himself that way, but at least it was better than drawing unfavorable attention and possible ridicule. Artists of various kinds—together with priests, ministers, and actors—were sometimes exceptions, but everybody knew they were a peculiar crowd anyhow.

When the old stereotypes began to break down in the middle of the twentieth century—a revolution crystalized in the musical *Hair*—it was of course a liberating experience for males just as for everybody else. Starting with the younger ones, they could put an earring in one ear and wear a pony tail without having their masculinity called into question. If they opposed war, violence, and nuclear power, they might get into trouble with the cops, but most people no longer considered them traitors to their gender. It was even acceptable for them to stay home and take care of the children while their wives went out to earn the family living.

Needless to say, males continue to be as much of a problem to themselves now that the sky's the limit as they ever were. Maybe moreso. With females more or less liberated right alongside them, they're not quite as much in charge as they used to be, and that leaves them feeling a little vulnerable and disoriented. Free to be almost anything these days, now they've got a harder time figuring out what to be. With everything pretty much up for grabs, they're not sure what's worth grabbing.

Father and Husband, Brother and Son, Lover and Friend—all the old roles are still there for them to fill, but with the old scripts discarded, they're left to ad lib it as best they can. It's the Prodigal all over again, off on his own in a far country and perishing with hunger for he's not sure what.

MARRIAGE

They say they will love, comfort, honor each other to the end of their days. They say they will cherish each other and be faithful to each other always. They say they will do these things not just when they feel like it but even—for better for worse, for richer for poorer, in sickness and in health—when they don't feel like it at all. In other words, the vows they make at a marriage could hardly be more extravagant. They give away their freedom. They take on themselves each other's burdens. They bind their lives together in ways that are even more painful to unbind emotionally, humanly, than they are to unbind legally. The question is: what do they get in return?

They get each other in return. Assuming they have any success at all in keeping their rash, quixotic promises, they never have to face the world quite alone again. There will always be the other to talk to, to listen to. If they're lucky, even after the first passion passes, they still have a kindness and a patience to depend on, a chance to be patient and kind. There is still someone to get through the night with, to wake into the new day beside. If they have children, they can give them, as well as each other, roots and wings. If they don't have children, they each become the other's child.

They both still have their lives apart as well as a life together. They both still have their separate ways to find. But a marriage made in Heaven is one where a man and a woman become more richly themselves together than the chances are either of them could ever have managed to become alone. When Jesus changed the water into wine at the wedding in Cana, perhaps it was a way of saying more or less the same thing.

ME

As in *me first* and *gimme,* the pronoun has gotten a bad name over the years. It's other people we're told we should be thinking about. It's giving to them. But taken all by itself—just *me*—there's something rather poignant about it. Only two letters long. Barely one syllable. It looks as though it needs all the help it can get.

"Love your neighbor as yourself," we're told. Maybe before I can love my neighbor very effectively, I have to love me—not in the sense of a blind passion but in the sense of looking after, of wishing well, of forgiving when necessary, of being my own friend.

MONEY

The more you think about it, the less you understand it.

The paper it's printed on isn't worth a red cent. There was a time you could take it to the bank and get gold or silver for it, but all you'd get now would be a blank stare.

If the government declared that the leaves of the trees were money so there would be enough for everybody, money would be worthless. It has worth only if there is not enough for everybody. It has worth only because the government declares that it has worth and because people trust the government in that one particular although in every other particular they wouldn't trust it around the corner.

The value of money, like stocks and bonds, goes up and down for reasons not even the experts can explain and at moments nobody can predict, so you can be a millionaire one moment and a pauper the next without lifting a finger. Great fortunes can be made and lost completely on paper. There is more concrete reality in a baby's throwing its rattle out of the crib.

There are people who use up their entire lives making money so they can enjoy the lives they have entirely used up.

Jesus says that it's easier for a camel to go through the eye of a

needle than for a rich man to enter the Kingdom of God. Maybe
the reason is not that the rich are so wicked they're kept out of the
place but that they're so out of touch with reality they can't see it's
a place worth getting into.

MOTHER

Jesus was by no means sentimental on the subject. He said that
people who loved their mothers more than they loved him were
not worthy of him (Matthew 10:37), indicating that duty comes
first. And when they told him his mother was outside waiting while
he spoke to some group or other, he said that his mother was anybody who did God's will (Matthew 12:50), indicating that his fel-
low believers came a close second.

To his own mother he could be very abrupt. When she came to
him at the wedding in Cana to tell him the wine had given out,
he said, "O woman, what have you to do with me? My hour has
not yet come" (John 2:4), meaning perhaps that she was to let him
alone, that at that early point in his ministry he wasn't ready to be
known as a miracle-worker. He was speaking his heart to her if not
exactly reprimanding her, and it was just woman he called her, not
mother.

Some of the last words he ever spoke were in her behalf, however. She was standing at the foot of his cross when he told her in
effect that from then on his disciple John would look after her.
"Behold your son," he said, indicating him to her (John 19:26).
Again it was just woman he called her, but her welfare and safe-
keeping were among the last thoughts he ever had.

Our mothers, like our fathers, are to be honored, the Good Book
says. But if Jesus is to be our guide, honoring them doesn't mean
either idealizing or idolizing them. It means seeing them both for
who they are and for who they are not. It means speaking the truth
to them. It means the best way of repaying them for their love is
to love God and our neighbor as faithfully and selflessly as at their

best our parents have tried to love us. It means seeing they are taken care of to the end of their days.

NAKEDNESS

Everybody knows what everybody else looks like with no clothes on, but there are few of us who would consider going around in public without them. It is our sexuality that we're most concerned to hide from each other, needless to say, although one sometimes wonders why. Males and females both come with more or less standard equipment after all. There would be no major surprises.

It started, of course, with Adam and Eve. Before they ate the apple, "the man and his wife were both naked, and were not ashamed," Genesis tells us, and it was only afterwards that "they sewed fig leaves together and made themselves aprons" (Genesis 2:25, 3:7). In other words, part of knowing Evil as well as Good was to know sex as a way of making objects of each other as well as a way of making love, and we have all felt guilty about it ever since. "Pudenda" deriving from the Latin for *that of which we ought to be ashamed* is etymology at its most depressing.

People go around dressed to the nines, and in our minds we go around undressing them. Again one wonders why. It's not just to see their bodies surely. We already know what those look like. If our most abandoned fantasies came true and we were actually to have our way with the bodies that attract us most, I suspect it wouldn't even be that either. We already know what just bodies can do and what they can't.

Maybe our hunger to know each other fully naked is in the last analysis simply our hunger to know each other fully. I want to know you with all your defenses down, all your pretenses set aside, all your secrets laid bare. Then maybe I will be brave enough to lay myself bare so that at last we can be naked together and unashamed.

NARCOTICS

Whether they make you feel silly or dreamy or bursting with cosmic energy, whether they induce euphoria or hallucinations, whether they give you a sense of being all-powerful and all-knowing or a sense of drifting through space like the dawn, they all offer you a temporary reprieve from reality. Needless to say, that's what makes narcotics in particular and drugs in general so addictive. Everybody wants out from time to time, and they provide a way. They provide an adventure. Most of all, maybe, they provide a vacation from being yourself.

It was Karl Marx who called religion the opiate of the masses, and the metaphor was not intended to be complimentary. Religion is only a way of making the poor forget the bitter reality of their life on earth by giving them pipe-dreams of pie in the sky by and by. That's what Marx meant by his comparison, and the history of the church has frequently confirmed his analysis. There are other ways of comparing them, however.

For instance, whereas people who do drugs get a temporary reprieve from a reality they often find too hard to live with, religious people claim to find a new kind of life grounded in a Reality they find increasingly hard to live without. They claim also that although narcotics may provide you with an adventure, the life of faith is an adventure in itself because once you start out on that path, there's no telling where it may take you next.

Finally they would say that if by dulling or sharpening or altering your senses you can get a vacation from being yourself, by coming to your senses you can little by little—often quite painfully at first but more and more gratefully as time goes by—become yourself. That much of the pie, anyway, can be yours this side of the sky.

NATURE

An unnatural mother means one who doesn't behave the way mothers are supposed to behave, and a natural affection is the kind of affection that's right on the mark, unlike the other kinds that make respectable flesh crawl just to think about them. When somebody does or is asked to do something abominable, you can say that it is against nature because nature is not abominable. Natural foods, natural colors, natural flavors, the natural look, and so on, are currently the advertising industry's highest endorsement. The idea of Mother Nature represents the same view of things—nature as nurturing, pure, beneficent, on the side of the good.

Unfortunately, Adam and Eve took nature with them when they fell. You've only to look at the sea in a November gale. You've only to consider the staggering indifference of disease, or the field at Antietam, or a cook boiling a lobster, or the statistics on child abuse. You've only to remember your own darkest dreams.

But the dream of Eden is planted deep in all of us too. A parade of goldenrod by the road's edge. The arc of a baseball through the summer sky. The way a potter's hand cradles the clay. They all cry aloud of the might-have-been of things, and the may-be-still.

NAVE

The nave is the central part of the church from the main front to the chancel. It's the part where the laity sit and in great Gothic churches is sometimes separated from the choir and clergy by a screen. It takes its name from the Latin *navis,* meaning ship, one reason being that the vaulted roof looks rather like an inverted keel. A more interesting reason is that the Church itself is thought of as a ship or Noah's Ark. It's a resemblance worth thinking about.

In one as in the other, just about everything imaginable is aboard, the clean and the unclean both. They are all piled in together helter-skelter, the predators and the prey, the wild and the tame, the sleek and beautiful ones and the ones that are ugly as sin. There are sly young foxes and impossible old cows. There are the catty and the piggish and the peacock-proud. There are hawks and there are doves. Some are wise as owls, some silly as geese; some meek as lambs and others fire-breathing dragons. There are times when they all cackle and grunt and roar and sing together, and there are times when you could hear a pin drop. Most of them have no clear idea just where they're supposed to be heading or how they're supposed to get there or what they'll find if and when they finally do, but they figure the people in charge must know and in the meanwhile sit back on their haunches and try to enjoy the ride.

It's not all enjoyable. There's backbiting just like everywhere else. There's a pecking order. There's jostling at the trough. There's growling and grousing, bitching and whining. There are dogs in the manger and old goats and black widows. It's a regular menagerie in there, and sometimes it smells to high Heaven like one.

But even at its worst, there's at least one thing that makes it bearable within, and that is the storm without—the wild winds and terrible waves and in all the watery waste no help in sight.

And at its best there is, if never clear sailing, shelter from the blast, a sense of somehow heading in the right direction in spite of everything, a ship to keep afloat, and, like a beacon in the dark, the hope of finding safe harbor at last.

NEUROTICS

A minister began to preach by saying, "To start with, I'm just as neurotic as everybody else," and there was apparently an all but audible sigh of relief from the entire congregation. Anxiety, depression, hypochondria, psychosomatic aches and pains, fear of things like heights and crowds—there's almost nobody who can't lay claim to at least a few of them. They involve an utterly fruitless expenditure of energy. They result in an appalling waste of time. Yet maybe there's something to be said for them anyhow.

Neurotics don't lose their sense of reality like people who think they're a poached egg or that somebody's going to blow poison gas under the door while they're asleep. You might even say that they have a heightened sense of reality. They sense everything that's really there and then some. They don't understand why the peculiar things that are going on inside their heads are going on, but at least they're more or less in touch with what's going on inside their heads and realize not only that they're peculiar themselves but that so are lots of other people. That's probably why neurotics are apt to be more sympathetic than most, and, unless their particular neurosis happens to be non-stop talking or anti-social behavior, why they make such good listeners.

You wouldn't want one of them operating on your brain or flying you across the Andes in a jet or in charge of things when there's a Red Alert, but when it comes to writing poems and novels or painting pictures or even preaching sermons, it's hard to beat them. Their overactive imaginations, which are a curse elsewhere, are a blessing there. Personally speaking, their oversensitivity may be their undoing, but professionally it's one of their strongest cards. They may see and hear and feel more than is good for them, but there's no question that, with the exception of their immediate families, it's good for everybody else.

"A thorn was given me in the flesh, a messenger of Satan, to harass me, to keep me from being too elated," Saint Paul wrote to his friends (2 Corinthians 12:7). Nobody knows just what the problem was that he was referring to, but you don't have to read many of his letters to suspect that he would have been among those who sighed with relief at the minister's opening confession. His violent swings of mood from deep depression to exaltation. His passionate likes and dislikes. His boasting. His dark sense of guilt. Almost certainly it was some sort of neurosis that was bugging him. Three times he prayed to God to get rid of it for him, he said, but God never did. Maybe it's not so hard to guess why.

A psychological cure would no doubt have greatly enriched Paul's own life at the time but would have greatly impoverished generations of his readers' lives ever since. "Through his wounds we are healed" are words to be reserved only for the most grievous Wound, the holiest Healing (Isaiah 53:5). But maybe in some small measure they can be applied to people like Paul too. Their very hang-ups and crotchets and phobias and general quirkiness give their kind—and through them give us—insights into the human heart that few can match. It's a high price for them to pay for our comfort and edification, but where they come closest to a kind of odd-ball holiness of their own is the feeling they give you some-times that even if they could get out of paying it, they wouldn't.

NEWS

When the evening news comes on, hundreds of thousands of people all over the earth are watching it on their TV screens or listening to it on their radios. Disasters and scandals, scientific breakthroughs and crimes of passion, the Cold War and all the smaller hot wars, negotiations that fail and others that succeed, the perpetual search for peace—people sit there by the millions half dazed by the things that go to create each particular day. Maybe they even try to make some kind of sense of it or, if they're not up to that, at least try to come to some sort of terms with it, try to figure out how it's apt to affect them for good or ill.

There is also, of course, the news that rarely if ever gets into the media at all, and that is the news of each particular day of each particular one of us. That is the news we're so busy making that we seldom get around to sitting down and thinking it over. If it takes some extraordinary turn we might, but the unextraordinary, commonplace events of each day as they come along we tend to let slip by almost unnoticed. That is, to put it mildly, a pity. What we are letting slip by almost unnoticed are the only lives on this planet we're presumably ever going to get.

We're all of us caught up in our own small wars, both hot and cold. We have our crimes and passions, our failures and successes. We make our occasional breakthroughs. God knows we are searching for peace. It's all apt to happen so quietly and on so small a scale we hardly realize it's happening. Only an unanswered letter. A phone conversation. A tone of voice. A chance meeting at the post office. An unexpected lump in the throat. Laughing till we cry. But these things are what it's all about. These things are what we are all about.

Maybe there's nothing on earth more important for us to do than sit down every evening or so and think it over, try to figure it out if we can, at least try to come to terms with it. The news of *our* day. Where it is taking us. Where it is taking the people we love. It is, if nothing else, a way of saying our prayers.

OBEDIENCE

In recent times "obedience" has become a bad word. It seems incompatible with good words like "independence," "individualism," and "freedom." The emphasis is all on doing your own thing and doing it your own way. What you're supposed to obey is authority, and authority has come to be confused with "the authorities"—people in uniform or with Ph.D.s or earning ten times a year more than you do. Who wants to obey *them?*

Many parents have given up asking their children to obey them and just hope they won't burn the house down. In religious circles, obedience, like its partners poverty and chastity, tends to be associated largely with monasticism. If the Mother Superior or the Abbot tells you to do something, you better do it. Otherwise you let your own conscience be your guide and take no guff from anybody. The phrase "obeying your conscience" is gradually being replaced by "listening to your conscience."

It is generally supposed that to obey somebody is necessarily to do something for somebody else's sake. That is a tragic misunderstanding. When Jesus asks people to obey above everything the Law of Love (q.v.), it is above everything for their own sakes that he is asking them to obey it.

OBSERVANCE

A religious observance can be a wedding, a christening, a Memorial Day service, a bar mitzvah, or anything like that you might be apt to think of. There are lots of things going on at them. There are lots of things you can learn from them if you're in a receptive state of mind. The word "observance" itself suggests what is perhaps the most important thing about them.

A man and a woman are getting married. A child is being given a name. A war is being remembered and many deaths. A boy is coming of age.

It is life that is going on. It is always going on, and it is always precious. It is God that is going on. It is you who are there that is going on.

As Henry James advised writers, be one on whom nothing is lost.

OBSERVE!! There are few things as important, as religious, as that.

OLD AGE

It's not, as the saying goes, for sissies. There are some lucky ones who little by little slow down to be sure but otherwise go on to the end pretty much as usual. For the majority, however, it's like living in a house that's in increasing need of repairs. The plumbing doesn't work right any more. There are bats in the attic. Cracked and dusty, the windows are hard to see through, and there's a lot of creaking and groaning in bad weather. The exterior could use a coat of paint. And so on. The odd thing is that the person living in the house may feel, humanly speaking, much as always. The eighty-year-old body can be in precarious shape yet the spirit within as full of beans as ever. If that leads senior citizens to think of all the things they'd still love to do but can't anymore, it only makes things worse. But it needn't work that way.

Second childhood commonly means something to steer clear of, but it can also mean something else. It can mean that if your spirit is still more or less intact, one of the benefits of being an old crock is that you can enjoy again something of what it's like being a young squirt.

Eight year olds like eighty year olds have lots of things they'd love to do but can't because their bodies aren't up to it, so they learn to *play* instead. Eighty year olds might do well to take notice. They can play at being eighty year olds for instance. Stiff knees and hearing aids, memory loss and poor eyesight, are no fun, but there are those who marvelously survive them by somehow managing to see them as among other things and in spite of all, a little funny.

Another thing is that if part of the pleasure of being a child the first time round is that you don't have to prove yourself yet, part of the pleasure of being a child the second time round is that you don't have to prove yourself any longer. You can be who you are and say what you feel, and let the chips fall where they may.

Very young children and very old children also have in common the advantage of being able to sit on the sideline of things. While everybody else is in there jockeying for position and sweating it out, they can lean back, put their feet up, and like the octogenarian King Lear "pray, and sing, and tell old tales, and laugh at gilded butterflies."

Very young children and very old children also seem to be in touch with something that the rest of the pack has lost track of. There is something bright and still about them at their best, like the sun before breakfast. Both the old and the young get scared sometimes about what lies ahead of them, and with good reason, but you can't help feeling that whatever inner goldenness they're in touch with will see them through in the end.

PATRIOTISM

All "isms" run out in the end, and good riddance to most of them. Patriotism for example.

If patriots are people who stand by their country right or wrong, Germans who stood by Adolf Hitler and the Third Reich should be adequate proof that we've had enough of them.

If patriots are people who believe not only that anything they consider unpatriotic is wrong but that anything they consider wrong is unpatriotic, the late Senator Joseph McCarthy and his backers should be enough to make us avoid them like the plague.

If patriots are people who believe things like "Better Dead Than

Red," they should be shown films of Hiroshima and Nagasaki on August 6 and 9, 1945, respectively, and then be taken off to the funny farm.

The only patriots worth their salt are the ones who love their country enough to see that in a nuclear age it is not going to survive unless the world survives. True patriots are no longer champions of Democracy, Communism, or anything like that but champions of the Human Race. It is not the Homeland that they feel called on to defend at any cost but the planet Earth as Home. If in the interests of making sure we don't blow ourselves off the map once and for all, we end up relinquishing a measure of national sovereignty to some international body, so much the worse for national sovereignty.

There is only one Sovereignty that matters ultimately, and it is of another sort altogether.

PLAY

When King David's wife berates him for making a fool of himself by leaping and dancing before the ark of the Lord with all his might, he protests by saying that it seemed exactly the right thing to do considering all the Lord had done for him. "Therefore will I play before the Lord," he tells her (2 Samuel 6:14–21).

When God describes how he will rescue Jerusalem from his wrath and make it new again, "a city of truth" (Zechariah 8:3), he conveys the glory of it by saying, "And the streets of the city shall be full of boys and girls playing in the streets" (Zechariah 8:5).

When the Psalmist praises God for creating "this great and wide sea, wherein are creeping things innumerable," he makes special mention of Leviathan, "whom," as he says, "thou hast made to play therein" (Psalm 104:25–6).

The king, the boys and girls, the whale—they are none of them accomplishing anything. They are none of them proving anything. There's nothing edifying or educational or particularly helpful in what they are doing, nothing that you'd be likely to think of as religious. They haven't a thought in their heads. They are just *playing,* that's all. They are letting themselves go and having a marvelous time at it.

David has sweat pouring down his face and his eyes aflame. The boys and girls are spinning like tops. The whale has just shot a thirty-foot spout into the air and is getting ready to heave his entire one hundred and fifty tons into the air after it.

What is the wind doing in the hayfield? What is Victoria Falls up to, or the surf along the coast of Maine? What about the fire going wild in the belly of the stove, or the rain pounding on the roof like the Hallelujah Chorus, or the violet on the windowsill leaning toward the sun?

What, for that matter, is God up to, getting the whole thing started in the first place? Hurling the stars around like rice at a wedding, gathering the waters together into the seas like a woman gathering shells, calling forth all the creatures of earth and air like a man calling Swing Your Partner at a hoedown.

"Be fruitful and multiply!" God calls, and creator and creature both all but lose track of which is which in the wonder of their playing.

POLITICS

You can't help wondering what would happen if a person running for the presidency decided to set politics in the sense of flag-waving, tub-thumping, axe-grinding, and the like aside and to speak instead candidly, thoughtfully, truthfully out of his or her own heart.

Suppose a candidate were to stand up before the reporters and the TV cameras and the usual bank of microphones and say something like this:

"The responsibilities of this office are so staggering that anybody who doesn't approach them with knees knocking is either a fool or a lunatic. The literal survival of civilization may depend on the decisions that either I or one of the other candidates make during the next four years. The general welfare and peace of mind of millions of people will certainly depend on them. I am only a human being. If I have my strengths, I also have my weaknesses. I can't promise that I'll always do the right thing for this country. I can only promise that it will always be this country rather than my own political fortunes that I'll try to do the right thing for. I believe in this country at its best, but I also believe that we have made many tragic mistakes. I believe this has been especially true in our dealings with the Soviet Union. Under the assumption that they will destroy us if we don't, we have spent untold billions on military defense that could have immeasurably improved the lot of all of us here at home. This has encouraged them to make the same assumption about us and to spend themselves blind as well. I am willing to entertain the possibility that our assumptions about them may be as wrong as their assumptions about us, and my major objective if elected will be to explore that possibility with them at the highest levels of government and in the most radical, searching, and unrelenting ways I can devise. I believe that the survival and well-being of the human race as a whole is more important than the partisan interests of any nation including both theirs and our own."

There are many who would undoubtedly say that such a statement is naive, dangerous, unrealistic, un-American, and that anybody making it couldn't get elected dog-catcher. I can't help believing, however, that there are others who would find it such a note of sanity, honesty, and hope in the political quagmire that they would follow the person who made it to the ends of the earth.

PSYCHOTHERAPY

After Adam and Eve ate the forbidden fruit, God came strolling through the cool of the day and asked them two questions: "Where are you?" and "What is this that you have done?" Psychotherapists, psychologists, psychiatrists, and the like have been asking the same ones ever since.

"Where are you?" lays bare the present. They are in hiding, that's where they are. What is it they want to hide? From whom do they want to hide it? What does it cost them to hide it? Why are they so unhappy with things as they are that they are trying to conceal it from the world by hiding, and from themselves by covering, their nakedness with aprons?

"What is this that you have done?" lays bare the past. What did they do to get this way? What did they hope would happen by doing it? What did they fear would happen? What did the serpent do? What was it that made them so ashamed?

God is described as cursing them then, but in view of his actions at the end of the story and right on through the end of the New Testament, it seems less a matter of vindictively inflicting them with the consequences than of honestly confronting them with the consequences. Because of who they are and what they have done, this is the result. There is no undoing it. There is no going back to the garden.

But then comes the end of the story where God with his own hands makes them garments of skins and clothes them. It is the most moving part of the story. They can't go back, but they can go forward clothed in a new way—clothed, that is, not in the sense of having their old defenses again behind which to hide who they are and what they have done but in the sense of having a new understanding of who they are and a new strength to draw on for what lies before them to do now.

Many therapists wouldn't touch biblical teachings with a ten-foot pole, but in their own way, and at their best, they are often following them.

QUEEN OF HEAVEN

The Greeks called her Artemis and the Syrians Atargatis. The Egyptians worshiped her as Isis and the Assyrians as Ishtar. In Jeremiah's day the women kneaded dough to make cakes in her likeness and burned incense to her. In the Book of Revelation she became "a woman clothed with the sun, with the moon under her feet, and on her head a crown of twelve stars" (Revelation 12:1). She is the goddess of heaven and earth who answers petitions, heeds sighs, and loves mercy. She is the lady of nurture and fertility who restores life to the earth at springtime.

In the Judeo-Christian tradition, God has been thought of largely as King, Father, Judge, Lord of Hosts, and the like, and these exclusively male metaphors testify to the experience of God as all-powerful, just, demanding obedience, benign, and so on. But there are other dimensions of the experience that they clearly leave out. Whatever else the Roman Catholics' adoration of the Virgin Mary may be, in this respect at least it helps restore the balance.

It is from the ancients that Rome borrowed the title they honor Mary with: *Regina Coeli,* or Queen of Heaven. God is Mother as well as Father—compassionate, forgiving, life-giving, endlessly creative and nourishing. She brings us forth from her womb. We take love at her breast.

QUIET

An empty room is silent. A room where people are not speaking or moving is quiet. Silence is a given, quiet a gift. Silence is the absence of sound and quiet the stilling of sound. Silence can't be anything but silent. Quiet chooses to be silent. It holds its breath to listen. It waits and is still.

"In returning and rest you shall be saved," says God through the prophet Isaiah, "in quietness and confidence shall be your strength" (Isaiah 30:15). They are all parts of each other. We return to our deep strength and to the confidence that lies beneath all our misgiving. The quiet there, the rest, is beyond the reach of the world to disturb. It is how being saved sounds.

RACISM

In 1957 when Governor Faubus of Arkansas refused to desegregate the schools in Little Rock, if President Eisenhower with all his enormous prestige had personally led a black child up the steps to where the authorities were blocking the school entrance, it might have been one of the great moments in history. It is heart-breaking to think of the opportunity missed.

Nothing in American history is more tragic surely than the relationship of the black and white races. Masters and slaves both were dehumanized. The Jim Crow laws carried the process on for decades beyond the Emancipation. The Ku Klux Klan and its like keep going forever. Politically, economically, socially, humanly the blacks continue to be the underdog. Despite all the efforts of both races to rectify the situation and heal the wounds, despite all the progress that has been made, it is still as hard for any black to look at any white without a feeling of resentment as it is for any white to look at any black without a feeling of guilt.

"There is neither Jew nor Greek, there is neither slave nor free, there is neither male nor female; for you are all one in Christ Jesus," Paul wrote to the Galatians (3:28), and many a white and many a black must have read his words both before the Civil War and since, perhaps even given them serious thought. If more whites had taken them to heart, were to take them to heart today, you can't help speculating on all the misery—past, present, and to come—that both races would have been spared.

Many must have taken them to heart but then simply not done what their hearts directed. The chances are they weren't bad people or unfeeling people all in all. Like Eisenhower, they simply lacked the moral courage, the creative vision that might have won the day. The Little Rock schools were desegregated in the end anyhow by a combination of legal process and armed force, but it was done without some gesture of courtesy, contrition, compassion that might have captured the imagination of the world.

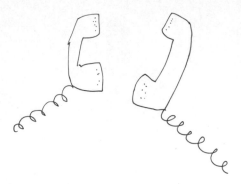

REMEMBER

When you remember me, it means that you have carried something of who I am with you, that I have left some mark of who I am on who you are. It means that you can summon me back to your mind even though countless years and miles may stand between us. It means that if we meet again, you will know me. It means that even after I die, you can still see my face and hear my voice and speak to me in your heart.

For as long as you remember me, I am never entirely lost. When I'm feeling most ghost-like, it's your remembering me that helps remind me that I actually exist. When I'm feeling sad, it's my consolation. When I'm feeling happy, it's part of why I feel that way.

If you forget me, one of the ways I remember who I am will be gone. If you forget me, part of who I am will be gone.

"Jesus, remember me when you come into your kingdom," the good thief said from his cross (Luke 23:42). There are perhaps no more human words in all of Scripture, no prayer we can pray so well.

SECOND COMING

Just before the final benediction, the New Testament ends with the prayer, "Come, Lord Jesus!" (Revelation 22:20). When he came the first time, he came so unobtrusively that except for Mary and Joseph and a handful of shepherds, nobody much knew or cared. But he says he will come a second time.

Who knows how he will come, or when, or where. He says himself, "Of that day and hour no one knows, not even the angels of heaven, nor the Son, but the Father only" (Matthew 24:36). People who in search of a timetable try to crack the Book of Revelation like a code are on a wild goose chase. People who claim that all who join their sect will be saved and all others lost are wrong. The ones who will be saved, Jesus says, are the ones who feed the hungry, welcome the stranger, clothe the naked, visit the sick and the prisoners (Matthew 25:31–46). If you love, in other words, you're in. If you don't, you're out. It doesn't seem to matter to him whether you're a Jehovah's Witness, a Jesuit, or a Jew.

In one of the more outlandish of his outlandish images, he says he will come like a thief in the night (Matthew 24:42–43). We must be ready at all times therefore. We can never be sure when he will break into the world like a house, when he will break into our lives.

No one can say just what will happen when that day comes, but that it will be a day to remember there is no doubt. The dead will be raised. The Last Judgment will take place. The present age will end and the new age begin. In Dante's vision, the redeemed will shine like a great white rose unfolding petal by petal in the light of glory. In John's, the new Jerusalem will come down out of Heaven like a bride.

"My grace is sufficient for you, for my power is made perfect in weakness," the risen Christ said to his servant Paul (2 Corinthians 12:9). It is in that hope only that we dare say Amen to the prayer that brings all Scripture to a close.

SEXUALITY (See HOMOSEXUALITY, NAKEDNESS.)

SLEEP

It's a surrender, a laying down of arms. Whatever plans you're making, whatever work you're up to your ears in, whatever pleasures you're enjoying, whatever sorrows or anxieties or problems you're in the midst of, you set them aside, find a place to stretch out somewhere, close your eyes, and wait for sleep.

All the things that make you the particular person you are stop working—your thoughts and feelings, the changing expressions of your face, the constant moving around, the yammering will, the relentless or not so relentless purpose. But all the other things keep on working with a will and purpose of their own. You go on breathing in and out. Your heart goes on beating. If some faint thought stirs somewhere in the depths of you, it's converted into a dream so you can go on sleeping and not have to wake up to think it through before it's time.

Whether you're just or unjust, you have the innocence of a cat dozing under the stove. Whether you're old or young, homely or fair, you take on the serenity of marble. You have given up being in charge of your life. You have put yourself into the hands of the night.

It is a rehearsal for the final laying down of arms, of course, when you trust yourself to the same unseen benevolence to see you through the dark and to wake you when the time comes—with new hope, new strength—into the return again of light.

STORY

It is well to remember what the ancient creeds of the Christian faith declare credence in.

God of God, Light of Light . . . for us and for our salvation came down from heaven . . . born of the Virgin Mary . . . suffered . . . crucified . . . dead . . . buried . . . rose again . . . sitteth on the right hand of God . . . shall come again, with glory, to judge both the quick and the dead. That is not a theological idea or a religious system. It is a series of largely flesh and blood events that happened, are happening, will happen, in time and space. For better or worse, it is a story.

It is well to remember because it keeps our eyes on the central fact that the Christian faith *always* has to do with flesh and blood, time and space. more specifically with your flesh and blood and mine, with the time and space that day by day we are all of us involved with. stub our toes on, flounder around in trying to look as if we have good sense. In other words, the Truth that Christianity claims to be true is ultimately to be found, if it's to be found at all, not in the Bible, or the Church, or Theology—the best they can do is point to the Truth—but in our own stories.

If the God you believe in as an idea doesn't start showing up in what happens to you in your own life, you have as much cause for concern as if the God you don't believe in as an idea does start showing up.

It is absolutely crucial, therefore, to keep in constant touch with what is going on in your own life's story and to pay close attention to what is going on in the stories of others' lives. If God is present anywhere, it is in those stories that God is present. If God is not present in those stories, then you might as well give up the whole business.

SUICIDE

The most famous suicide in the Old Testament is King Saul's. He was doing battle with the Philistines. The Philistines won the day. They killed his three sons, and he himself was wounded by archers. Fearing that he would be captured by the enemy and made a mockery of if he survived, he asked his armor-bearer to put him out of his misery. When the armor-bearer refused, he fell on his own sword (1 Samuel 31:4).

Judas Iscariot's is of course the most famous one in the New Testament. When Jesus was led off to Pilate and condemned to death, Judas took his thirty pieces of silver and tried to return them to the Jewish authorities on the grounds that Jesus was innocent and he had betrayed him. The authorities refused to take them. They said that was his problem, and Judas, throwing the silver to the ground, went off and hanged himself (Matthew 27:3–5).

Taking your own life is not mentioned as a sin in the Bible. There's no suggestion that it was considered either shameful or cowardly. When, as in the case of Saul and Judas, pain, horror, and despair reach a certain point, suicide is perhaps less a voluntary act than a reflex action. If you're being burned alive with a loaded pistol in your hand, it's hard to see how anyone can seriously hold it against you for pulling the trigger.

TEARS

You never know what may cause them. The sight of the Atlantic Ocean can do it, or a piece of music, or a face you've never seen before. A pair of somebody's old shoes can do it. Almost any movie made before the great sadness that came over the world after the Second World War, a horse cantering across a meadow, the high school basketball team running out onto the gym floor at the start of a game. You can never be sure. But of this you can be sure. Whenever you find tears in your eyes, especially unexpected tears, it is well to pay the closest attention.

They are not only telling you something about the secret of who you are, but more often than not God is speaking to you through them of the mystery of where you have come from and is summoning you to where, if your soul is to be saved, you should go to next.

TODAY

It is a moment of light surrounded on all sides by darkness and oblivion. In the entire history of the universe, let alone in your own history, there has never been another just like it and there will never be another just like it again. It is the point to which all your yesterdays have been leading since the hour of your birth. It is the point from which all your tomorrows will proceed until the hour of your death. If you were aware of how precious it is, you could hardly live through it. Unless you are aware of how precious it is, you can hardly be said to be living at all.

"This is the day which the Lord has made," says the 118th Psalm. "Let us rejoice and be glad in it." Or weep and be sad in it for that matter. The point is to see it for what it is because it will be gone before you know it. If you waste it, it is your life that you're wasting. If you look the other way, it may be the moment you've been waiting for always that you're missing.

All other days have either disappeared into darkness and oblivion or not yet emerged from it. Today is the only day there is.

TOUCH

I hear your words. I see your face. I smell the rain in your hair, the coffee on your breath. I am inside me experiencing you as you are inside you experiencing me, but the you and the I themselves, those two insiders, don't entirely meet until something else happens.

We shake hands perhaps. We pat each other on the back. At parting or greeting, we may even go so far as to give each other a hug. And now it has happened. We discover each other to be three-dimensional, solid creatures of reality as well as dimensionless, airy creators of it. We have an outside of flesh and bone as well as an inside where we live and move and have our being.

Through simply touching, more directly than in any other way, we can transmit to each other something of the power of the life we have inside us. It is no wonder that the laying on of hands has always been a traditional part of healing or that when Jesus was around, "all the crowd sought to touch him" (Luke 6:19). It is no wonder that just the touch of another human being at a dark time can be enough to save the day.

TOURIST PREACHING

English-speaking tourists abroad are inclined to believe that if only they speak English loudly and distinctly and slowly enough, the natives will know what's being said even though they don't understand a single word of the language.

Preachers often make the same mistake. They believe that if only they speak the ancient verities loudly and distinctly and slowly enough, their congregations will understand them.

Unfortunately, the only language people really understand is their own language, and unless preachers are prepared to translate the ancient verities into it, they might as well save their breath.

TRANSFIGURATION

"His face shone like the sun," Matthew says, "and his garments became white as light." Moses and Elijah were talking to him. There was a bright cloud overshadowing him and out of it a voice saying, "This is my beloved son, with whom I am well pleased; listen to him." The three disciples who witnessed the scene "fell on their faces, and were filled with awe" (Matthew 17:1–6).

It is as strange a scene as there is in the Gospels. Even without the voice from the cloud to explain it, they had no doubt what they were witnessing. It was Jesus of Nazareth all right, the man they'd tramped many a dusty mile with, whose mother and brothers they knew, the one they'd seen as hungry, tired, footsore as the rest of them. But it was also the Messiah, the Christ, in his glory. It was the holiness of the man shining through his humanness, his face so afire with it they were almost blinded.

Even with us something like that happens once in a while. The face of a man walking his child in the park, of a woman picking peas in the garden, of sometimes even the unlikeliest person listening to a concert, say, or standing barefoot in the sand watching the waves roll in, or just having a beer at a Saturday baseball game in July. Every once and so often, something so touching, so incandescent, so alive transfigures the human face that it's almost beyond bearing.

UNBELIEF

Unbelief is as much of a choice as belief is. What makes it in many ways more appealing is that whereas to believe in something requires some measure of understanding and effort, not to believe doesn't require much of anything at all.

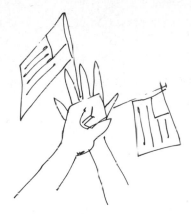

U.S.A.

The Ku Klux Klan and the Bill of Rights. *Moby Dick* and drug-store paperbacks. Abraham Lincoln and Warren Gamaliel Harding. The Mississippi River and Coney Island. Reinhold Niebuhr and Jim Bakker. Vietnam and the Peace Corps.

Out of many, one. The question, of course, is: one what? The hope of the world? The despair of the world?

Anybody who lived through the Cuban Missile Crisis of 1962 is unlikely to forget it. The U.S.S.R. refusing to call back its freighters. The U.S.A. refusing to call off its blockade. The world going to sleep at night wondering if there would be a world to wake up to in the morning.

One misstep is all it would have taken. One misstep is all it will take.

VANITY

Vanity is futility.

According to the Book of Ecclesiastes, everything is vanity because the good and the evil, the wise and the foolish, the lucky and the unlucky, the have and the have-nots, all turn to dust in the end. If you're honest about it, that's a hard point to refute.

Saint Paul puts it this way, "If Christ has not been raised, then our preaching is in vain and your faith in in vain. . . .If for this life only we have hoped in Christ, we are of all people most to be pitied" (1 Corinthians 15:14, 19). In other words, he is as honest as Ecclesiastes if not more so. But then he goes one step further.

He says Christ *has* been raised. In honesty he has to say that too because on his way to the city of Damascus one day he experienced it. That being so, he suggests, not even death is futile. That being so, not even life is in vain.

VIRTUE

Next to the Seven Deadly Sins, the Seven Cardinal Virtues are apt to look pale and unenterprising, but appearances are notoriously untrustworthy.

Prudence and *temperance* taken separately may not be apt to get you to your feet cheering, but when they go together, as they almost always do, that's a different matter. The chain smoker or the junkie, for instance, who exemplifies both by managing to kick the habit, can very well have you throwing your hat in the air, especially if it happens to be somebody whom for personal reasons you'd like to have around a few years longer. And the *courage* involved isn't likely to leave you cold either. Often it's the habit-kicker's variety that seems the most courageous.

If you think of *justice* as sitting blindfolded with a scale in her hand, you may have to stifle a yawn, but if you think of a black judge acquitting a white racist of a false murder charge, it can give you gooseflesh.

The *faith* of a child taking your hand in the night is as moving as the faith of Mother Teresa among the untouchables, or Bernadette facing the skeptics at Lourdes, or Abraham, age seventy-five, packing up his bags for the Promised Land. And *hope* is the glimmer on the horizon that keeps faith plugging forward, of course, the wings that keep it more or less in the air.

Maybe it's only *love* that turns things around and makes the Seven Deadly Sins be the ones to look pale and unenterprising for a change. Greed, gluttony, lust, envy, pride are no more than sad efforts to fill the empty place where love belongs, and anger and sloth just two things that may happen when you find that not even all seven of them at their deadliest ever can.

WISDOM

In the Book of Proverbs, Wisdom is a woman. "The Lord created me at the beginning of his work," she says (Proverbs 8:22). She was there when he made the heaven, the sea, the earth. It was as if he needed a woman's imagination to help him make them, a woman's eye to tell him if he'd made them right, a woman's spirit to measure their beauty by. "I was daily his delight, rejoicing before him always," she says (Proverbs 8:30), as if it was her joy in what he was creating that made creation bearable, and that's why he created her first.

Wisdom is a matter not only of the mind but of the intuition and heart, like a woman's wisdom. It is born out of suffering as a woman bears a child. It shows a way through the darkness the way a woman stands at the window holding a lamp. "Her ways are ways of pleasantness," says Solomon, then adding, just in case there should be any lingering question as to her gender, "and all her paths are peace" (Proverbs 3:17).

WOMAN (See DEPRESSION, FEMALE, QUEEN OF HEAVEN, WISDOM.)

WORK

If you lose yourself in your work, you find who you are.
If you express the best you have in you in your work, it is more than just the best you have in you that you are expressing.

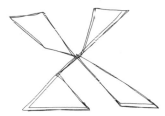

X-RATED

The terms Adult Books, Adult Movies, Adult Entertainment imply that whereas the young must be somehow protected from all those bare breasts and heaving buttocks, adults will simply take them in their stride. Possibly the reverse is closer to the truth.

The young seem to have a knack for coming through all sorts of heady experiences relatively unscathed, and paperback prurience and video venery are less apt to turn them on than to turn them elsewhere. The middle-aged, on the other hand, having fewer elsewheres, settle for what they can get.

After the first half hour or so, the X-rated titillations tend to turn tawdry and tedious, but even days later, they keep on flickering away somewhere in the back of the mind to a captive audience of one.

The chances are that the loneliness and sadness of it then may leave deeper scars on the forty-five-year-old than the gymnastics of it on a thirteen-year-old child.

YOU

In the Book of Genesis, the first word God speaks to a human being is *you* (Genesis 2:15), and in the Book of Revelation, the last word a human being speaks in effect to God is "Come, Lord Jesus!" which is to say "Come, *you!*" (Revelation 22:20).

It is possible that the whole miracle of Creation is to bridge the immeasurable distance between Creator and Creature with that one small word, and every time human beings use it to bridge the immeasurable distances between one another, something of that miracle happens again.

YOUTH *(See also* ADOLESCENCE, CHILDHOOD, OLD AGE.)

Youth isn't for sissies either.

ZERO

"In the beginning . . . the earth was without form and void, and darkness was upon the face of the deep" (Genesis 1:1–2). In other words, God started with nothing, zero, and out of it brought everything.

In the end, says John, "I saw a great white throne and him who sat upon it; from his presence earth and sky fled away, and no place was found for them" (Revelation 20:11). In other words, there is zero again, and out of it God brought a new heaven and a new earth.

Perhaps more than for anything else, God is famous for calling something precious out of something that doesn't even exist until he calls it. At the beginning of each one of us it happened, and at the end of each one of us maybe by God's grace it will happen again.

DATE DUE

NOV 8 1988	
AUG 1 4 1990	
SEP 1 3 1990	
AUG 1 1991	
MAY 0 5 1993	
APR 1 1 1996	

| UPI 261-2505 | PRINTED IN U.S.A. |